THE WEALDEN
IRON INDUSTRY

T0333778

THE WEALDEN IRON INDUSTRY

JEREMY HODGKINSON

For Sue

First published 2008

Reprinted 2009, 2011
The History Press
The Mill, Brimscombe Port
Stroud, Gloucestershire, GL5 2QG
www.thehistorypress.co.uk

British Library Cataloguing in Publication Data.
A catalogue record for this book is available from the British Library.

ISBN 978 0 7524 4573 1

Typesetting and origination by The History Press
Printed in Great Britain

CONTENTS

PREFACE

The Weald of Sussex, Kent and Surrey is a distinct region, defined by its geology and its landscape. It had a reputation for impenetrability; Rudyard Kipling, who loved it and made it his home for 34 years, called it the 'secret' Weald. Looking across the Wealden countryside, from any vantage point, it is hard to recognise elements which suggest that it was once an industrial landscape (*colour plate 1*). Yet, for about 2000 years the Weald supported an iron industry; and for two distinct periods – during the first part of the Roman occupation and in the Tudor and early Stuart periods of our history – it was the principal iron-producing region in Britain. For within that landscape are all the raw materials necessary for the production of iron: clay and sandstone for building, clay ironstone ore, wood for fuel and construction, and water for power. Four hundred and fifty years ago, nearly 100 furnaces and forges roared and hammered in the Weald, while smoke curled up from as many woods or more, and roads were busy with the passing traffic of wagons laden with ore, charcoal, iron sows and cannon. It was an industry that drew upon and affected the entire economy of the Weald; it provided employment and created wealth, yet it despoiled the land with pits and slag heaps; above all, it has bequeathed a legacy of peaceful woodlands, of beautiful houses and fine expanses of water, of curious place names, and of ancient relics in churchyard and hearth.

Less than 25 years have passed since the publication of the last major study of the iron industry in the Weald, and this book is not intended to supersede that exceptional work. Rather, this is an attempt to present the story of the industry in a less academic form, for the more general reader. My close involvement with Wealden iron has, however, provided me with the opportunity to include discoveries and new research not available to earlier writers. This book which, for reasons of length, omits much detail, should be read in conjunction with those works that have preceded it, not in place of them.

In the preparation of this book, I am indebted to many people. In particular I must mention Reg Houghton with whom, over more than 30 years, I have spent many happy hours discussing pretty well every aspect of the iron industry, and who has generously executed many of the diagrams and drawings for this book. I am equally grateful to Roger Bourne, of Arka Cartographics Ltd. of Forest Row, whose unsolicited offer to draw the maps was a great kindness. Dot Meades and Tony Fellows willingly agreed to read through drafts of this book; their comments and suggestions have been of great help. No blame attaches to them for the text that has resulted; it is mine alone. I owe particular thanks to my son, Tom, for the loan of his camera, without which many of the illustrations would not have been possible to obtain, and to Christopher Whittick, of East Sussex Record Office, for sourcing maps for me from its collection. Those images are reproduced by kind permission of the County Archivist and depositors. For allowing me to take and/or use photographs of objects in their care or possession I must thank Mr and Mrs Christopher Jermyn, Mrs Anne Norris, Mr and Mrs Derek Yeats, Mr and Mrs John Wallace, Ann Callow and Graham Price, Robin Hodgkinson, David Pinnegar, Mrs A. Ward and Pam White of Squerryes Court, Roy Calthorpe and the Trustees and Committee of Battle Museum of Local History, East Grinstead Town Council, the Trustees of East Grinstead Museum, Crawley Museum Society, and the incumbents of several Wealden parish churches. Dot Meades, Sarah Paynter, Charles Trollope, David Butler, Chris Butler, Sue Howard, Bernard Worssam and Simon Stevens have kindly allowed me to reproduce their photographs or drawings, as have the Sussex Archaeological Society, Dover Publications Inc., the National Portrait Gallery, West Sussex Record Office and the Centre for Kentish Studies.

Finally I must express my gratitude to my many friends and colleagues in the Wealden Iron Research Group, whose stimulating company has been a great encouragement to me, and whose generosity has permitted me to use photographs and drawings from its publications.

Jeremy Hodgkinson
January 2008

1

GEOLOGY AND RAW MATERIALS

The geology of the Weald is predominantly clay and sandstone, and from them many of the structural needs of the iron industry could be met. It is in the clay that the ironstone can be found. The same clay was used to make bricks, not only for domestic and agricultural buildings, but also parts of blast furnaces and forges. Clayey sand was used to make the primitive furnaces operated from pre-Roman times until the end of the Middle Ages. More resilient sandstone provided the hearths and outer walls for the blast furnaces that were introduced at the end of the fifteenth century.

The structure of the Weald resulted from a long process whereby a series of sedimentary rocks, formed of sands, clays and limestones, were laid down, one above the other over what we now recognise as south-eastern England and north-eastern France. Tens of millions of years later, huge movements in the Earth's crust caused Africa to collide with Europe, and the Alps to become uplifted. These tremendous forces sent ripples across northern Europe, which folded the layers laid down earlier. One of these major ripples lifted the beds laid down where the Weald is, causing a dome. However, as fast, in geological terms, as this dome, or anticline, rose, erosion wore it away, removing the younger rocks, like chalk and greensand, and gradually exposing the older layers in the centre of the dome (*1*). The oldest of these is known as Ashdown Sand, which forms the highest ground in the centre of the Weald. Lying above that is the Wadhurst Clay, with Tunbridge Wells Sand above that. These Hastings Beds, as they are called, constitute what is known as the High Weald. The landscape which arises from these strata is characterised by undulating ridges and small valleys. The streams which pass through these valleys, forming the headwaters of the Mole, Medway, Rother, Cuckmere, Ouse, Adur and Arun, flow away from the centre of the Weald, even cutting through the North and South Downs on their way to the sea. That the Wealden rivers do this is proof of their great antiquity, for it indicates that they have been in existence from early on in the process that caused the Wealden anticline to rise. Around

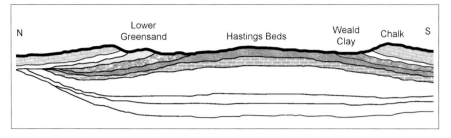

1 Simplified cross-section of the geology of the Weald (*after R. Gallois*)

the High Weald is a clay lowland called the Low Weald (*2*). Composed of the Weald Clay, it is much flatter country. The sandstones in the High Weald give rise to distinctive sunken lanes, while the clays result in heavy soils which are difficult to farm.

THE GEOLOGY OF IRON ORE

The sandstones and clays which form the Weald were deposited in marshy, flood-plain conditions during the Cretaceous period, between 120 and 140 million years ago. Sediments eroded from older geological formations contained dissolved iron minerals which were probably consolidated by microbial action and began to form ironstones. The conditions in which these processes were able to occur lasted only for brief periods in relation to geological time, and for long intervals iron deposition did not occur at all, causing a succession of thin layers of ore to be laid down, often in patches. The main formations of iron ore occur as clay ironstone in several of the strata of the Wealden series. They occur as nodules or thin flat masses most notably in the lower levels of the Wadhurst Clay, but also in clay bands in the Ashdown Sand and Tunbridge Wells Sand as well as in the Weald Clay. The nodules, which are formed of an iron carbonate called siderite (*colour plate 2*), are distinctive in that weathering causes them to develop a dark skin or crust of hydrated iron oxide called limonite. The quantities of ironstone, or mine as it was called, were never large by modern standards, occurring in bands up to about 15cm thick. Each layer varied in age and, because of the different conditions when it was laid down millions of years ago, it varied in quality (*3*). Some ores were formed of a limestone comprising the fossil shells of a small bivalve mollusc called *cyrena* (*colour plate 3*). The charge fed into a modern blast furnace includes a percentage of limestone, the inclusion of which makes the iron separate more effectively from the waste material, or slag. Wealden iron-makers seem to have been aware of the specific qualities of this limestone, reckoning it a type of ore, and recognised that its inclusion was essential in the charge of a furnace.

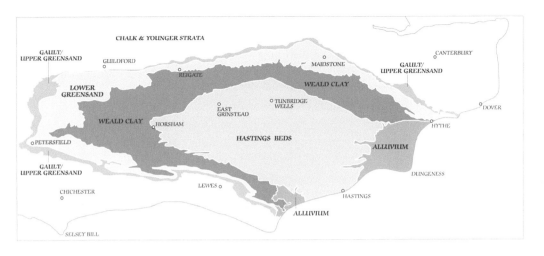

Above: 2 The geology of the Weald, simplified (*R. Bourne*)

Right: 3 Section of Wadhurst Clay in a minepit at Sharpthorne, showing successive layers of ore (*after B. Worssam*)

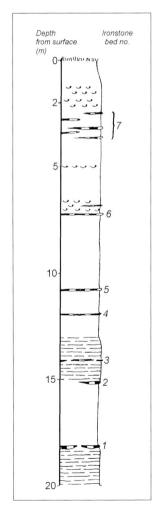

The distribution of iron ore throughout the Weald varies according to the rock strata. In the High Weald, while the Ashdown Sand lies lowest in the geological sequence, with the Wadhurst Clay and then the Tunbridge Wells Sand successively above that, the outcropping of these layers is confused by complex folding and faulting caused by the Alpine tectonic movements over 60 million years ago. Thus the occurrence of iron ore is far from predictable, with layers sometimes appearing on one side of a valley and not on the other, or the strata dipping down steeply so that miners could only extract ore along a narrow swathe of countryside before it became too deep and the quantity of overburden was too great. On the Weald Clay the ore outcrops more regularly, though the number of layers is fewer. Two main sequences of ore occur in the Weald Clay: lower in the geological sequence, just above the Tunbridge Wells Sand, and higher up, that is more recent, just below the Lower Greensand. This latter layer was the principal source of ore for the furnaces that were established in the west of Sussex, around Petworth. More recent concentrations of iron ore are still being formed as masses of varying size in the subsoil of poorer-drained areas of the Weald, on the clay vales of south Surrey, west Sussex and west Kent. This is sometimes known as shrave or pudding stone.

IRON ORE MINING

It is likely that the earliest ironworkers derived their ore from natural exposures of the mineral in stream banks, digging back into the ground and removing the layers of nodules as required. On a number of early sites, such excavations have been found and more extensive opencast quarries have been noticed near to larger sites of prehistoric and Roman date. In some cases such workings must have sustained sites for many years: at Beech Wood, north of Sedlescombe, an opencast working adjacent to the Footland Farm Iron Age and Romano-British bloomery site has slag scattered over its floor, indicating that early iron smelting operations continued after the quarry was exhausted as a source of ore. A larger quarry lies further up the hillside. In the Roman period, when all mineral rights were vested in the Imperial administration, it may not have mattered unduly how much the landscape was damaged by such workings. By the Middle Ages, however, when land ownership had become well established in the Weald, the despoiling of the ground by ore digging and the resultant reduction in agricultural land is likely to have caused more concern. From this period, ironstone extraction was more often carried out by digging shafts, known locally as minepits because the name at that time for the ore was mine (4). These pits would have been refilled using the waste contents of the succeeding pit. Radiocarbon dates from the late twelfth and thirteenth centuries, derived from pieces of wood

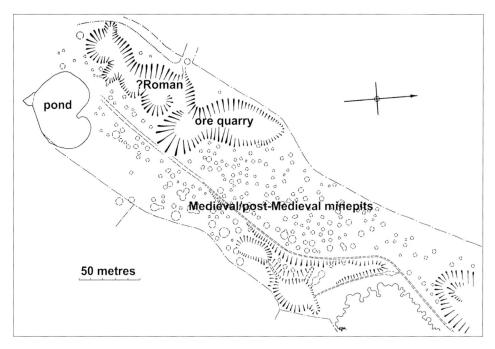

4 Ore pits in Tugmore Shaw, Hartfield, showing opencast quarries (probably Roman) and later shaft minepits (*R. Houghton*)

found in the fill of minepits sectioned by modern brickearth extraction at Sharpthorne, showed that the pits were refilled more than 800 years ago, and that iron-making was active nearby at that time. By refilling the pits the ground could be restored to some use, such as woodland. In time, however, the fill of these pits settled, resulting in a distinctive landscape in which areas of ground became pockmarked with shallow, saucer-shaped depressions. These are often filled with water in wet weather and have given rise to place names such as Minepit Wood.

From the sixteenth century onwards, digging or drawing mine became a large-scale operation as the demand for ore increased. Gangs of labourers toiled in the intractable clay. Probably two men would dig a pit – taking it in turns to dig, or to shovel the clay and ore into buckets or baskets – with a third man at the surface hauling up the material with a simple winch, and either filling a previously dug pit with the surplus clay, or loading the ore into a wagon or into panniers on horses (5). Pits could be as much as 12m deep, averaging 5m across. Often they were no more than 5m apart. There is no evidence that they were extended sideways at the bottom, although sometimes the pits were dug so close together, that they eventually merged into a larger hole, or the ground between earlier pits was reworked. On digging each pit several layers of ore would be encountered, and it is likely

5 Eighteenth-century ore digging (*from The Universal Magazine November 1764*)

that the ore from the different layers would be kept separate from each
other so that founders could take advantage of their different properties.
Contemporary accounts refer to 'fine', 'coarse', 'greys' and 'pitty' mine, and
the Heathfield ironmaster, John Fuller, wrote that 'the skill of the Founder
doth very much consist in knowing the certain quantity of each sort [of ore],
that he may make good iron'. Visiting Barden furnace near Speldhurst in
1646, Sir James Hope, a Scottish lead producer, identified separate heaps of ore
of four different varieties, each with distinctive colours and characteristics. It
seems unlikely that the demand for ore for the 113 furnaces recorded in the
Weald could have been satisfied from supplies derived from shaft minepits
alone. Evidence points to open-cast quarries providing a significant source
of ore for some furnaces: a few hundred metres upstream from Queenstock
furnace, Buxted, probably the earliest furnace in the Weald, Minepit Wood
may be just such a source. Within living memory a quarry used for ore
extraction, adjacent to the site of Warren furnace, near Crawley Down, was
filled in. However, shaft minepits continued to be used to gain iron ore: as
late as 1767, William Clutton, a former ironmaster and by then steward of
the manor of Broadhurst, near Horsted Keynes, was advising his employer
that those who were seeking to dig for ore on his land should 'fill the holes
up in the proper manner'.

ORE ROASTING

Iron-makers found it beneficial to pre-roast the iron ore before smelting. Also known as calcining or elyng, ore roasting had the effect of converting the ore from a carbonate to an oxide, which made it easier to reduce in the furnace. It also dried out the ore and broke it into smaller pieces. All of these made it easier for the gases in the furnace to permeate the ore and produce the desired chemical effect more efficiently. Roasted ore is a distinctive soft, dark red mineral which is attracted to magnets (*colour plate 4*). Roasting was carried out on open fires, using wood or charcoal as a fuel, probably building up successive layers of fuel and ore. Although examples of roasted ore are commonly found in excavations, evidence of ore roasting sites has been found relatively rarely. This may be because excavators have concentrated their efforts on the main working areas of sites – the furnaces and forges – and roasting was more likely to have been carried out some distance from the smelting areas, perhaps for safety reasons. The smoke, and the tendency of the roasting ore to burst and spit in the fire, were both inconvenient and hazardous. At Little Furnace Wood, Mayfield, a Romano-British bloomery of the first and second centuries AD, ore roasting was carried out about 75m from the smelting furnaces in large, shallow pits 3-4m square (*6*). In the fourteenth century, a stone platform was constructed for ore roasting at Minepit Wood bloomery, Rotherfield, outside the walled enclosure where smelting took place (*7*). Less is known of the extent to which ore roasting was carried out at post-medieval blast furnaces. Sir James Hope observed ore roasting heaps at Barden furnace, where charcoal was gradually mixed with the ore and added to the fire, thus working through each heap. He described the burning heap as 'lyeing in disorder and … not in any kill [kiln]'. Accounts of Ashburnham furnace, which itemise payments in considerable detail in the latter part of the eighteenth century, make no mention of ore roasting, so it is likely that the practice varied from furnace to furnace, possibly according to the quality of the ore, and that at some it was not carried out at all.

The amount of iron ore needed to produce a quantity of iron varied both in time and from place to place. However, comparisons are difficult because of the different ways used to measure quantities. In the post-medieval period, ore was measured by volume, in loads, basically the amount contained in a wagon. Output, however, was measured by weight. So there is an immediate problem in equating one measure with the other. As a rough guide, about three tons of ore produced one ton of iron in a blast furnace, where reduction of the ore into molten iron and slag was virtually total. In earlier times, when iron was smelted in bloomeries, the proportions would have been rather different because a considerable percentage of the iron was lost into the slag. Experiments in smelting iron by primitive methods have shown that it takes as much as 10 times as much ore as will be output in iron, although it can be

6 Romano-British ore-roasting pit at Little Furnace Wood, Mayfield (*C. Butler*)

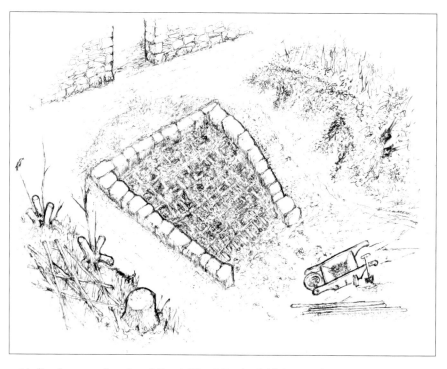

7 Medieval ore-roasting pit at Minepit Wood, Rotherfield (*R. Houghton*)

reasonably expected that early iron-makers were probably more proficient and used less ore than modern experimenters. The cost of ore as a proportion of the expenditure of an ironworks also varied with the passage of time. Due to bloomeries consuming rather more ore in relation to their output of iron than blast furnaces did, the cost of the ore at the Tudeley ironworks in Kent in the fourteenth century averaged at about 12 per cent of the total annual expenditure of the works. Four centuries later, at Ashburnham, it accounted for only about 9 per cent of the costs.

CHARCOAL

A prevailing feature of the Weald is its woodland; Sussex remains one of the most heavily wooded counties in England. Much of the tree cover in the Weald is a legacy of the iron industry, for charcoal was always the fuel which kept the furnaces and forges alight. Evidence from the analysis of charcoal found on excavated sites is that the most frequently used type of wood in bloomery furnaces in the Iron Age and Roman periods was oak, although hazel and birch were also common. This is not surprising as these species are among the most abundant in the Weald. With the majority of sites in this period being modest in scale, early ironworkers would have been able to satisfy their demand for wood to make charcoal by cutting down small trees or using fallen branches, but when demand increased, some management of wood resources would have been necessary. It is not unreasonable to assume that some form of woodland management was essential to satisfy the demand for charcoal for some of the larger ironworks of the Roman period, but no evidence has survived. In the accounts of the ironworks that belonged to Lady Elizabeth de Burgh, at Tudeley in Kent in the fourteenth century, the source of the charcoal – whether coppiced or free-growing – is not specified. Wood for ore roasting, or *elyngwood*, is itemised, as is *olwood*, which may be fallen branches. The works purchased most of the charcoal it needed from the Southfrith estate. It was delivered in units called *decena*, or tens, for the first years of the accounts, although this changed to *duodena*, or dozens. The quantities seem to relate to packhorse loads. A *duodena* of charcoal made about five and a half blooms of iron; a bloom being the product of one smelt, although its precise weight is not known.

When the use of the blast furnace began to spread during the sixteenth century, fears were expressed that the Weald would become deforested and that other trades would be affected. Iron-makers, up until then, had been used to drawing upon sustainable local resources of wood for their bloomeries, which probably consumed, at most, about 10 tons of wood a year. The introduction of blast furnaces and finery forges (see Chapter 4) increased charcoal consumption by as much as 100 times for each ironworks, and as the number of furnaces increased, large areas of woodland were being cut down. Writers at the time bemoaned the loss of woodland, but the extent to which they were overstating the situation continues to be debated. Some writers have pointed to examples of deforestation where, within a generation, areas formerly named as woods were being referred to as commons instead. And it was not just underwood that was being cut down. In their desperate efforts to obtain enough wood to feed furnaces that burned as much as a ton of charcoal a day, full-grown trees were being felled. Other writers have pointed to the practical problems that ironmasters would have experienced in over-felling and in using unsuitable timber, and suggested that contemporary commentators might have had protectionist motives for seeking to restrict the spread of iron-making in the Weald. It is no surprise that, with wood being a staple product for a huge range of needs, whether domestic, craft or industrial, competition for the woodland resources of the Weald was intense and, many felt, unfair. In 1548 the authorities in the coastal towns petitioned the Crown to call a halt to the seemingly insatiable appetite of the furnaces, and a commission was set up to examine the complaints. Among these objections were that the ironworks were taking wood that was needed for export to Calais for fuel, that there was no longer sufficient wood for building or for making household goods, and that:

8 Modern coppicing near Midhurst

if the iron mills continue only there shall be but a few take commodity by them, and many a thousand not yet born feel with their parents the great hurt and incommodity engendered by their continuance.

HMC Salisbury MSS, XIII (HMSO, 1915)

Perhaps they protested too much. The government responded in the fullness of time with an Act of Parliament in 1559 that restricted the setting up of new ironworks within 14 miles of the sea – except in Sussex, the Weald of Kent and in the parishes of Charlwood, Newdigate and Leigh in Surrey. However, the ironmasters themselves were beginning to feel the pinch. Having stripped bare large tracts of the countryside, they were running up against a shortage of wood. Significantly a later Act, which renewed the restriction on the expansion of the iron industry in Surrey and Kent, pointed to an example of good practice which encouraged others to follow. Christopher Darrell, a Kent ironmaster but operating a furnace at Ewood in Surrey, was singled out in the Act and exempted from its restrictions, because of the way in which he had introduced coppicing and managed the woodland to supply his ironworks.

The practice of coppicing, whereby trees were cut down to their base and then allowed to regrow in several separate shoots, not only prevented wholesale loss of woodland but also provided the basis for long-term, sustainable wood supply (8). The regular cutting of underwood actually encouraged the growth of large standard trees, wood from which was suitable for building houses and ships, because it enabled the larger trees to grow at a sufficient distance apart for their branches to develop fully above the coppice wood. The wood used most often for charcoal for iron-making was oak, birch and beech; hazel and, latterly, hornbeam were also used, and it had to be allowed to regrow for at least fifteen years before it could be coppiced again. This length of time was necessary because the wood stems needed to be of sufficient diameter, and therefore strength, when made into charcoal, to bear the weight of the iron ore in the furnace. Otherwise it would be crushed to powder and the smelt would fail. With charcoal burners restricted to harvesting coppice wood for iron-making only every 15 years, cutting of woodland had to be rotated, and it has been calculated that as much as 2500 acres of coppice would have been needed to supply a blast furnace over such a period. Added to that, the finery forge, which was a secondary process necessary in the production of wrought iron, required a further 1500 acres over the same period. Thus the demand for wood in the late sixteenth century, when there were 100 furnaces and forges active in the Weald, was enormous, with a quarter of the land area within a three mile radius of a furnace and forge needing to be coppiced. The demand for wood by each ironworks made it necessary to secure woodland not only within easy reach of the works, to avoid the charcoal having to undergo a long, bumpy and potentially destructive journey to the furnace or forge, but also avoiding direct competition with neighbouring works (9). Thus

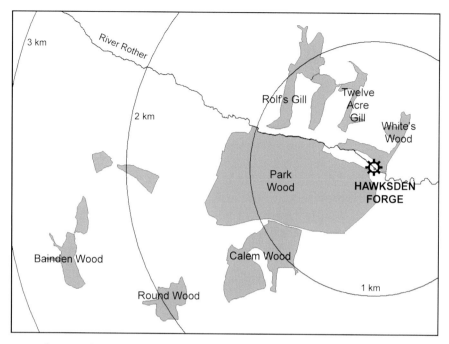

9 Wood sources for Hawksden forge, Mayfield, in the eighteenth century, showing distances from the forge

Robertsbridge furnace and forge drew their wood supplies from south of the River Rother, while the woods to the north of the river provided charcoal for Iridge furnace. Gentlemen's agreements probably ensured that one ironworks did not try to obtain supplies from the area around another.

The time it took to grow placed a premium on such coppice and made it more expensive, for landowners could reasonably expect to get a faster return on their woodland if was coppiced for other uses, such as fence posts or, in later years, hop-poles. However, the quality of the soils in the Weald was poor and rents were low, so woodland remained commercially viable for landowners. The supply of charcoal was the most expensive element in the cost of iron-making because of the labour-intensive nature of the work and the variety of costs which were included. Although some ironmasters had freehold of the land from which they were able to draw their supplies of wood, particularly in the earlier part of the sixteenth century, when it was the major landowners who were establishing ironworks, the majority had to obtain supplies from the land belonging to neighbouring owners. As the number of furnaces and forges increased, competition for the right to cut wood became more intense and prices rose. Having secured the woodland, skilled charcoal burners, or colliers as they were also known, were then brought in to cut and coal the wood. The accounts of some ironworks itemise in detail the individual operations that needed to be carried out. At Ashburnham furnace in the 1760s, the clerk had to pay a series of charges: felling the trees; cording them, which involved cutting them into shorter lengths (usually about 4ft or 1.2m) and piling them in stacks called cords; cleaving the larger lengths into more manageable sizes for burning; carting the wood, where necessary, to a central burning place; coaling, or burning, the wood; stacking the charcoal; carting the charcoal to the ironworks; and carting sacks of charcoal dust. The bark was generally stripped off the tree trunks for use in the tanning industry. Charcoal-burning clamps had to be built, lit and covered with turf, then supervised night and day. Then the charcoal had to be put in sacks and taken to the ironworks. The accounts of Ralph Hogge's ironworks in the 1570s mention the use of wood chips for smelting. This was a more expensive alternative to charcoal, probably because it was more difficult to use and less efficient.

As with ore, charcoal was measured in loads, so the same problems confront attempts to calculate the amount of charcoal needed to make a quantity of iron. Again, as a rough guide, varying accounts of charcoal consumed at ironworks from the sixteenth to eighteenth centuries can be rounded to about four loads to make a ton of cast iron in a blast furnace. Charcoal was also used as fuel in finery forges where an additional four loads of charcoal would be needed to convert cast iron sows into a ton of wrought iron.

2

IRON-MAKING BY
THE DIRECT PROCESS

BLOOMERIES

From prehistoric times until the end of the medieval period in the Weald, iron was made in small furnaces called bloomeries. A bloomery was a sandy-clay structure, which was cylindrical, dome-shaped or a combination of the two. It was open at the top for putting in the ore and charcoal, and had one or more holes in the side to allow air to be pumped in by hand. By heating the charcoal, using the bellows to raise the temperature, then adding the ore and regularly adding more charcoal and ore, the iron gradually became separated from the other minerals in the ore. The chemical process which caused the smelting resulted from the hot carbon monoxide gas (CO), produced by the burning charcoal, melting the ore and allowing the oxygen in the iron oxide (Fe_2O_3) to separate and combine with the CO to form carbon dioxide (CO_2). As the separation occurred, the other minerals in the ore, such as silica, which are known as the gangue, melted. The iron collected in a mass, called a bloom, near the bottom of the furnace, while the rest of the ore formed a semi-liquid slag, which ran down inside the furnace, and was either allowed to flow out of the furnace periodically, or collected in a pit beneath the furnace (*10 & 11*). After several hours the bloom was removed from the furnace and then consolidated, by gentle hammering, to expel any slag remaining in it, and formed into a solid piece of metal. The design of the furnace may have dictated how the bloom was removed. The bloom usually attached itself to the side of the furnace below the tuyere – the hole through which the air was pumped in – so it had to be dislodged before removal and either lifted out of the furnace from above, or pulled from within the furnace through a hole made at the front, perhaps where slag was allowed to run out. Undoubtedly it was easier to start to consolidate the bloom immediately after smelting had finished and while it was still hot; evidence survived at one of the bloomeries at Little Furnace Wood, Mayfield, of a small hearth immediately in front of the furnace, containing charcoal and small angular pieces of slag which were consistent with the bloom being consolidated there. At other smelting sites that have been excavated, similar hearths have been observed. However, slag derived from forging has been found at several sites in parts of Sussex some distance from the smelting areas of the Weald, which indicates that blooms may have been brought to these sites cold and then reheated later. Once the bloom had been consolidated it could be forged into a bar or other object. Although bars of forged bloomery iron have been found on archaeological sites in many parts of Britain, examples from the Weald are rare. This process, by which workable iron could be produced in a single stage, is known as the direct process of iron-making.

Bloomery furnaces have been found in many different forms, although the basic principle of their operation remained the same. Two basic types seem to have been used in the Weald, although exact comparisons are difficult because of the often poor survival of the upper parts of the furnace structure. What generally survives in excavated remains are the ground features, which take the form of either an elongated bowl, or depression, set into the ground or into a bank. Alternatively remains of what appear to have been free-standing structures, with little or no disturbance to the ground, have also been noted. While it was once thought that the developed bowl type of furnace was characteristic of native iron-making traditions, and the free-standing 'shaft' type indicated Roman influence, the range of furnace types found at the Iron Age/Romano-British site at Broadfield, Crawley, suggests that there was no clear chronological development of the form of bloomery furnaces, nor were there distinct geographical distributions of one or other type of furnace. Some excavated bloomeries have survived in remarkable condition; those at Minepit Wood, Rotherfield and in Little Furnace Wood, Mayfield, are good examples (*colour plates 5 & 6*). However, none has survived intact and it is often at the front of the furnace, perhaps where it is weakened by the tapping hole or where the bloom has been removed, that significant parts of surviving structures are most often missing.

One aspect of ancient bloomery remains which continues to be a cause for debate is the means of introducing the air needed to raise the furnace temperature. A few examples of fragments of tuyeres, the short clay tubes through which the blast of air was blown, have survived though not usually in their original positions in the furnace structure (*12*). Common finds on bloomery sites are short cylindrical pieces of slag, usually about 100mm long and between 10 and 20mm in diameter. They appear to have been formed by slag running into a tube and progressively blocking it for, in some instances, there is a small void in the middle of one end of the cylinder. It has been suggested that they were formed when holes were pierced in the front of a bloomery to allow the slag to escape. The only dated sites on which these objects have been found are from the Roman period. The amount of air

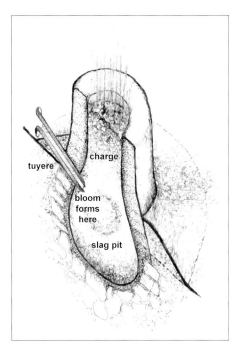
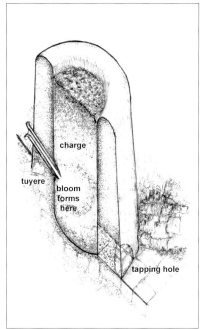

Above left: 10 Artist's reconstruction of a bloomery furnace with a slag pit (*R. Houghton*)

Above right: 11 Artist's reconstruction of a bloomery furnace from which slag could be tapped (*R. Houghton*)

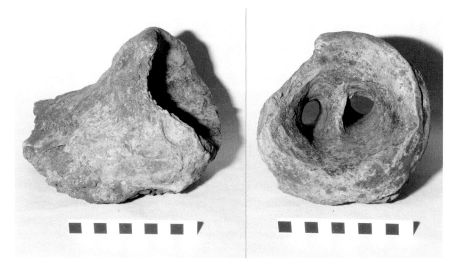

12 Romano-British clay double tuyere found at Bardown, near Wadhurst (scale 10cm)

13 Artist's reconstruction of Romano-British bloomery furnaces at Little Furnace Wood, Mayfield (*R. Houghton*)

that needed to be artificially forced into a bloomery varied according to its height. A tall structure might be capable of inducing a natural draught strong enough to raise the temperature high enough to allow smelting to take place. The poor survival of the upper parts of bloomeries means that we do not know how tall they were. Evidence from one of the furnaces in Little Furnace Wood, Mayfield, indicated that a cylindrical shaft or chimney about 500mm in diameter was built on top of the domed structure; similar contemporary remains have been excavated in France (*13*).

The waste slag, which had little further use, was discarded in heaps, and it is this which provides the best evidence for the existence of bloomery sites. To date, over 600 sites of early iron-making have been identified in the Weald. Many of them are small sites which were probably in operation for only a few seasons, but a few have thousands of tons of slag accumulated over many decades of production. On most bloomery sites the evidence of the slag tells us that the furnaces were of the type where slag was tapped regularly to allow more room in the furnace for further charges of ore and charcoal. Typical tap slag generally forms flat masses with 'worm-like' flow patterns on the upper surface, and an impression of the ground it has flowed over underneath (*colour plate 7*). However, in a minority of sites the only slag found suggests that it has flowed downwards, and the impressions of pieces of wood that it has flowed over are sometimes seen, the drips of slag indicating the direction of flow (*colour plate 8*). Furnaces producing this sort of slag may have been built with a slag pit beneath, into which the slag was allowed to flow, rather than allowing it to be tapped. To prevent the charge of charcoal and ore dropping straight into the pit during the early stages of smelting, the pit would be filled with sticks, which would partially burn away and through which the slag would drip.

At the time of writing, about 29 per cent of all the known bloomery sites have been dated, usually only approximately, to one or other of the main historical periods. The greatest number has been associated with the Roman occupation, which lasted from AD 43-410 (*14*). Dating is most easily achieved by excavating a small trench into the slag heap, where it is likely that domestic rubbish may have been left. This avoids damaging any structures, such as hearths, which might yield important environmental evidence, but offers a good chance of recovering datable pieces of pottery. A few sites have been fully excavated and have revealed remains of furnaces and other hearths, as well as evidence of buildings.

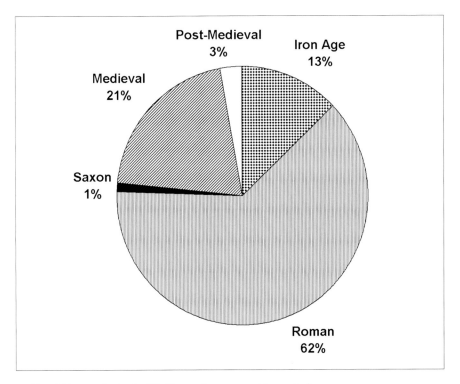

14 Dated bloomeries in the Weald; 113 sites arranged by period

PREHISTORIC IRON-MAKING

After Julius Caesar had visited Britain in 55 and 54 BC he wrote in his account
of his campaigns that iron was made in the coastal parts of the country. With
no other iron-making areas in Britain of that period close to the coast, it is
almost certain that he was referring to the Weald. A small number of bloomery
sites have revealed evidence of Iron Age pottery, predominantly from the first
and second centuries BC and the early first century AD (15). A problem which
dogs the identification of pre-Roman sites is the use, from the Late Iron Age
well into the Roman period, of native forms of pottery, particularly the type
known as East Sussex Ware. With little variation in the forms of this pottery
over a long period, it is hard to state with certainty, on the evidence of this
pottery type alone, whether a site is Late Iron Age or Romano-British. This
is compounded when, as is often the case, this type of pottery is the only type
found on many ironworking sites. Radiocarbon analysis, where available, can
provide a more accurate means of dating, but even with this technique some
results derived from sites in the 1960s and 70s, which seemed considerably at
odds with the evidence of pottery, have raised doubts as to its accuracy. It is,
therefore, with some caution that two recently obtained radiocarbon dates
should be viewed. The first resulted from the chance discovery of the remains
of a smelting hearth unearthed on Tablehurst Farm, Forest Row. Buried
1m below the surface, a charcoal sample sealed within the remains yielded
a date between AD 30 and 370 BC. At a less confident level, this could be
narrowed down to between the late third century and the mid first century
BC, putting the site early in the accepted time span of ironworking in the pre-
Roman period. However, only about 6km to the north-east, the discovery of
unfamiliar slag prompted the dating of charcoal from a trial excavation trench
in Cullinghurst Wood, Hartfield. The broad dating calibration produced a
surprising range from 350-750 BC, and less confidently at around the fifth
century BC, considerably earlier than anything in the Weald hitherto. Further
investigation will be needed to corroborate such a date.

     From the point of view of excavated remains, the most important of the
pre-Roman sites was the one at Broadfield, Crawley. The original report on
the dig there was not published, the records of the finds and their contexts
being inadequate or missing, and the final report had to be compiled, many
years later, from this less-than-perfect archive. What is clear is that the site
was being occupied from the second century BC and throughout the Roman
period. Evidence of a number of wooden buildings had been found, and
more than 60 bloomery furnaces were uncovered, of a variety of forms
which appeared neither to show any evolution from one type to another, nor
demonstrate an increasing sophistication following the Roman occupation.
Broadfield lies at the western extremity of the iron-producing district of that
time, and may possibly have been located there to supply the area further to

15 Iron Age bloomery sites in the Weald (*R. Bourne*)

the west, where the presence of iron ore was possibly not known then. Most
sites which operated in the Iron Age lie further to the east. Caesar's remark
about the coastal source of iron suggests one or two sites near Hastings which
are known to have been active in the first century BC. Some of the pottery
found at the large bloomery site near Footland Farm, Sedlescombe, has been
positively ascribed to the pre-Roman period, with strong evidence that it
continued operating during the course of the occupation. A similar state of
affairs applied to the site in Crowhurst Park, 7.5km to the south. Our present
knowledge of the distribution of smaller ironworking sites in the pre-Roman
period suggests no significant pattern, and the problems with dating lend
uncertainty as to what kind of organisation may have existed at the time.

In some instances pre-Roman ironworking has been associated with fortified
enclosures. At Garden Hill, Hartfield, at least one of the smelting furnaces may
be of the Late Iron Age. Other such sites where evidence of ironworking, though
not necessarily smelting, has been found include Dry Hill, near Lingfield,
Saxonbury, near Frant, and Piper's Copse, near Northchapel. The last of these
is considerably distant from other iron-making areas. A matter for some
speculation, but no firm conclusions, lies in the extent to which the distribution
of ironworking in the Weald in the Iron Age, and the variation in the technology

employed, was influenced by tribal affiliation. The territory of the *Cantiaci*, normally associated with Kent, probably included part of eastern Sussex. Similarly, the *Atrebates*, whose homeland included the north Hampshire-western Surrey area, seem to have extended their influence over parts of northern Sussex, including the Broadfield site, where eastern Atrebatic pottery was found. To the south of their lands their possible successors, the *Regni*, occupied territory east from Chichester. In each case, the extent of their respective influence or control over the Wealden area is unclear. The majority of the smaller sites likely to have been working in the pre-Roman period are subject to the provisos about dating already referred to. Some may have been active early in the Roman period and not been subject to Roman influence. The smelting furnaces at Minepit Wood, Rotherfield, at Turners Green, Warbleton, and at Smythford, Worth (this last being one where slag may not have been tapped during smelting) have been dated to this late period. Of possible significance are several small sites which have recently been identified in the Weald Clay area of the Vale of Kent, around Biddenden, Ulcombe and Smarden.

What is clear is that a relatively small number of sites were operating in the pre-Roman Weald, and that it is likely there were others although identification is difficult. Their output, at least in some cases, was sufficient to be noted by the Romans so that, when they arrived in Britain in the middle of the first century AD, they were able to build upon, and exploit, existing skills, and knowledge of the resources available.

IRON-MAKING IN THE ROMAN PERIOD

The occupation of Britain by the Romans, which began in AD 43, had a major effect on iron-making in the Weald. The modest industry that existed in the region in the Iron Age served as the nucleus for expansion over the next century. The iron-making skills of the native inhabitants of the Weald could be profitably employed by the Romans, iron being a material that was in demand for both civilian and military purposes. Evidence suggests that the Romans made use of the skilled native workforce by allowing them to continue using their own methods, and a number of sites with features encountered in pre-Roman contexts have produced dates which indicate they were operating in the Roman period. It is likely that the two coastal sites at Footlands and Crowhurst Park, which Julius Caesar may have been referring to in his account of his campaign in Gaul, were made use of early in the occupation. As the Romans acquainted themselves with the resources of the region, they began to organise how they would exploit the iron further inland. Imprecise dating of many of the bloomery sites, together with the frequent use of native pottery types common both before and after the Roman conquest, make it difficult to be certain which sites were in use early in the occupation.

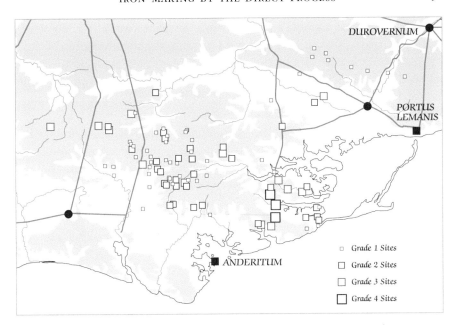

16 Romano-British bloomery sites, graded by estimated slag volume (*R. Bourne*)

At the time of writing, 113 ironworking sites in the Weald have been dated to the Roman period. They vary in size enormously, the largest possibly having produced as much as 3000 times more than the smallest (*16*). An estimate has been made of the quantity of slag at each of the Romano-British sites. This has been carried out, where possible, by multiplying the area of slag found at each site by an estimate of the average depth of the slag. As there would be a direct connection between the amount of slag and the amount of iron produced, the data derived from this study could be used to compare production at different sites and suggest a total for the Weald as a whole. Using these calculations, it has been found that 48 per cent of the sites had slag estimated at less than 100m³ each, representing a modest output produced during an operating period of a few seasons. A further 32 per cent of sites had slag heaps estimated at between 100m³ and 1000m³. These would have been occupied, probably seasonally as well, but for a longer period. Both groups of sites are fairly evenly distributed across the central High Weald. A smaller group – some 16 per cent – where the slag amounted to between 1000m³ and 10,000m³, and operation can be assumed to have been carried on over a period of several decades, are scattered more widely across the Weald. Finally, a small cluster of very large sites, only 4 per cent of the total, are concentrated in the south-east of the region. The total estimated slag volume for all the sites was over 148,000m³. Looking at each group of sites in turn, in relation to that total, the smallest group accounted for only 2 per cent of the total slag output, and the next group a mere 10 per cent, despite accounting for 80 per cent of all the sites. The remaining 20 per cent of the sites produced 88 per cent of the total output. This suggests that the majority of iron in the Weald in the Roman period was produced at no more than about 20 sites.

Apart from the large slag heaps at these important sites, many of them have revealed other indications as to their importance. At 25 of them high-status Samian pottery has been found. Evidence of building masonry has been found at a small number of sites, including Beauport Park and Chitcombe, as well as at Oldlands where several graves were noted. A large range of pottery has been found at Great Cansiron, near Hartfield. Lack of information about other large sites is generally because no excavation has been undertaken there.

So what was the role of the smaller sites? Many years ago the theory was put forward that they acted as satellites to the larger ones; an idea that seems to be supported by the distribution outlined above. Clearly several of the satellite sites could have been in existence for many years, judging by the quantity of slag which accumulated at some of them. Ironworking may have been a seasonal activity, with workers revisiting sites annually, dividing their time between iron-making and agriculture, for example. The two different bloomeries found at Little Furnace Wood, Mayfield, a site of only modest scale, suggest that the personnel responsible for making iron there changed during its working life, with one furnace-builder being replaced by another over the course of time.

The layout of Roman ironworking sites varied considerably, not only in scale, as has been discussed above, but also in the type of location. Many, however, occupy what may be regarded as a typical position (17). Although the ore used on such sites was drawn from the clay, bloomery sites are often found on sand. This may be because that subsoil provides a much drier base for the working area. It may also be because the raw material for furnace construction was sand with a small percentage of clay. The various elements of a site were organised in a downhill direction, with the ore source commonly on higher ground (the Wadhurst Clay naturally overlies the Ashdown Sand). Ore roasting would take place down the slope from the ore pits but at a sufficient distance from the main working area because of the thick smoke that often results from the green wood used to heat the ore. The furnaces were often built on a level area ranged along the top of a bank which dropped down to a stream. This allowed an easy way of disposing of the waste slag, by tipping it over the bank and preventing a build-up on the working area which might interfere with movement about the site. Forging would have been carried out close to the furnaces. The stream itself was useful. Water was not as essential in the iron-making process as it was to become in the post-medieval period, but it was beneficial, nevertheless, in the construction of furnaces, for washing, and in case of emergencies.

It has been suggested that the Romans set aside the Weald as an Imperial Estate, in which only industrial activities were to take place. Although there is no direct evidence that this happened, the fact that the Weald is one of the few areas in lowland Britain which is more than 25km from a Roman town, and that hardly any settlement can be associated with the region which does not

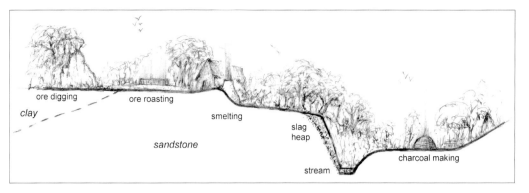

17 Cross-section of a typical Romano-British bloomery site in the Weald (*R. Houghton*)

have an industrial connection, marks out the Weald as an area which was not typical. The considerable increase in the number of ironworking sites in the region from those identified in the preceding period indicates that the Romans encouraged production both by the native ironworkers and also their own people. In addition to sites continuing in operation from before the conquest, as at Broadfield, Crowhurst Park and Footlands, several new sites were established, such as those at Oldlands, near Maresfield, Great Cansiron, in Hartfield, and Chitcombe, at Brede (*colour plate 9*), which were to become major production centres. Around them smaller sites came and went; many of them probably operated as satellites to the main sites. Within 50 years of the invasion, iron-making in the Weald was in full swing.

Added impetus was given to the industry with the involvement of the *Classis Britannica*. This was the British Fleet, and it was set up to facilitate the development of the new province of Britannia by acting as transportation across the Channel, carrying troops around the coast, and managing the supply of essential raw materials, such as wood, stone and iron. With its headquarters at Boulogne (*Gesoriacum*), and its British base at Dover (*Dubris*), the fleet began operations at the beginning of the second century and within a few years had become associated with at least three locations in the Weald. Those known are at Beauport Park, near Battle, Bardown, near Wadhurst, and at a site near Cranbrook. The centre of its operations in the Weald was probably at Beauport Park where a substantial bath-house has been discovered. Evidence of the fleet's activities comes in the form of locally manufactured roofing tiles stamped with the letters CLBR, and such tiles have been found at several other locations in the south of England (*colour plate 10*). It has been suggested recently that the presence of stamped tiles resulted merely from their carriage as ballast on returning vessels or wagons that had been used to transport iron. However, the fact that both iron and tiles were from inland sources that were geographically close, and that wagons returning to ironworking sites would not have been deliberately burdened with unnecessary freight, makes the suggestion implausible. Naturally,

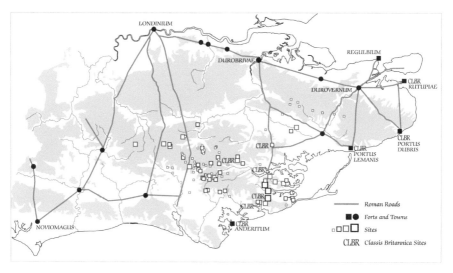

18 Classis Britannica sites and Roman communications in south-east England (*R. Bourne*)

the fleet would have used water as the main means of transporting the iron out of the Weald, so the discovery of the evidence of possible ports at Bodiam, along the route of the Roman road north from Beauport Park, and on the edge of the Pevensey levels, near Ninfield, where CLBR tiles have also been found recently, suggests departure points for local output. There are several other large Roman ironworking sites in the vicinity of Beauport and Bodiam, and although fleet involvement has not been proven there, it is very likely that such evidence may show up in the course of time (*18*). It has been estimated that the site at Beauport may have produced as much as 10,000 tons of iron in the century and a half before the fleet's role changed and it seems to have withdrawn from the exploitation of the iron resources in the Weald.

The Roman road that passed north from near Hastings has already been referred to. Sections of Roman roads that traversed the Weald were surfaced using the slag from ironworking, which was ideally suited to the purpose. The majority of the Roman roads crossing the Weald headed towards London, which is not without significance for the iron industry, for where all those roads met was at Southwark, just south of the bridging point across the Thames. Then a cluster of river islands, Southwark was a major centre of metalworking in both iron and other metals in the Roman period. No iron smelting seems to have been carried on there, but it is very probable that the bulk of the iron blooms that would have provided the raw material for the smiths there would have been brought up those roads from the Weald.

Despite the drop in output that inevitably followed the end of operations by the *Classis Britannica*, iron continued to be produced on a few sites in the Weald for the next 150 years until the end of the Roman occupation.

3

MEDIEVAL IRON-MAKING

For a long time after the Romans left Britain at the beginning of the fifth century there is no evidence of iron-making in the Weald. Why this is so is not known, for the people who lived there cannot have stopped using iron. It is possible that with the Romans exploiting the Weald less during the latter part of their occupation of the province, traditional skills passed down through the generations of native workers were lost. It is also possible that those who possessed iron-making skills migrated, or were relocated by the Romans, from the Weald to other areas of Britain, such as the Midlands or the South West, to develop iron production there.

The earliest site of medieval ironworking in the Weald is the Middle Saxon bloomery site at Millbrook, on Ashdown Forest, and it is unique in the Weald both for the primitive level of technology evident in the remains, and as the only smelting site known from the period. Discovered by chance during the laying of a pipeline, the remains were of a simple bowl-shaped furnace from which the upper parts were missing. Relining of the furnace indicated that it had been used for a small number of seasons; a small hearth for reheating the bloom, and a heap of slag, lay nearby. Radiocarbon and archaeomagnetic dating showed the furnace had been operated in the ninth century AD. The contrast in technology compared with the furnaces being used during the Roman period four centuries earlier reinforces the view that iron-making traditions had not survived into the Saxon period in the Weald. In fact, the type of furnace shows similarities with one excavated in the eastern Netherlands, which dated to a slightly earlier period. This hints at the possibility that the people using the furnace found at Millbrook were using technology introduced from the Saxon homelands, and that the descendants of the iron-makers in the Weald in the Iron Age and Roman periods had been displaced or had left; the lack of Celtic place names in the Weald supports this. It seems hard to believe that the Millbrook site could have been the only furnace of the Saxon period to have existed, but it is the only one to have been confirmed in the region from a period which lasted for 500 years. A bloomery site in Long Gill, Mayfield, has been radiocarbon dated to between 315 and 785 AD, which places it into the Saxon period, but there is no other evidence that confirms this dating.

The existence of other smelting sites in the Saxon period is suggested by discoveries indicating that that iron blooms were being forged on settlement sites. Excavations at Friar's Oak, just north of Hassocks, and at Buriton, near Petersfield in Hampshire, have produced evidence of such activity, but both are situated close to the South Downs, rather than being in the areas where smelting was likely. The site at Hassocks, at which there was also Roman material present, produced a quantity of slag from what appears to be the second stage of the iron-making process – the consolidation of the raw bloom – but no actual evidence of smelting. The scarp foot areas were the most densely and productively occupied in the early Saxon period; the Weald, both in the Kentish 'dens' and the manorial outliers of central western Sussex, being used initially, at any rate, for summer grazing. Settlements looking for an inexpensive source of iron for the manufacture and repair of their farm tools could have done worse than encourage their herders to make good use of a relatively idle time looking after grazing animals, by smelting the local iron ore. Concentrating on the smelting process, to save time, the small number of individuals who could have been spared would have been able to produce a respectable number of blooms in a season and carry them back to the home village for consolidating and forging during the winter months. The resulting products would have been able to satisfy their own needs, and provide a useful currency for exchange.

The site at Buriton was like the one at Hassocks in two significant ways: it was near the scarp foot, and it dated from the Middle Saxon period. The period is important because after that, towards the Late Saxon period, settlements would have increasingly become established in the Weald itself, and what iron was produced there would have been smelted, consolidated and forged *in situ*. Incidentally, it should be remembered that the Millbrook site dated from the same period as both Hassocks and Buriton, and may represent just such a location, where seasonal herdsmen turned their hands to metalwork. This type of activity may well have had its precursors in the Romano-British period, for it is hard to explain all of the increasing number of small ironworking sites as satellites of larger ones. The discovery of ironworking remains from the same stage in the production process as those at Hassocks, but from the Roman period, at a site at Burgess Hill, in Sussex, lends support to this theory.

Moving forward in time to the late eleventh century, there is only one reference to ironworking in the Weald in the Domesday Book. A forge, described in Latin as *una ferraria*, in an unnamed manor near to East Grinstead, Sussex, is unlikely to have been merely a smithy, as these would have been commonplace in agricultural communities. This is supported by the fact that only two other such holdings feature in the Domesday Book in the south-east of England: at Stratfield Turgis in north Hampshire, and at Chertsey in Surrey. Recent work has suggested a plausible identification of the Sussex manor, one of a group clustered around the headwaters of the Medway. The holding, known as Lavertye, just north of Forest Row, conforms to the size of the manor held by Ansfrid, and formerly by King Edward the Confessor. It had once been an outlier of Ditchling, a manor at the foot of the escarpment of the South Downs, and may, too, have owed its origin to seasonal working of the type suggested above. The fact that the manor, in common with the *ferraria* at Stratfield Turgis, had been a possession of the king is intriguing and attaches additional significance to this site. Searches of the area have failed, so far, to uncover its location.

A few miles to the west of Lavertye is an area of iron mining at Sharpthorne, near West Hoathly. Modern brick clay extraction exploiting the Wadhurst Clay has exposed shaft minepits that had been dug to extract a series of layers of ore. The area of pits is typical of many throughout the Weald: shallow, saucer-shaped depressions, the result of shafts being dug and then refilled. The exposure of sections of these pits not only enabled measurements to be taken of the depth and diameter of the workings, but also material deposited during the refilling of the pits could be examined for dating evidence. The expectation was that the pits dated from the post-medieval period and were dug to provide ore for one of several blast furnaces operating in the area. It was a surprise, therefore, when part of a tree trunk, and a piece of roughly squared and mortised timber that had been recovered from the fills of two pits, produced radiocarbon dates of AD 1220+/-80 and AD 1120+/-75 years respectively. The implication of these dates, which suggest that the pits were probably dug towards the end of the twelfth century, is that more than one medieval bloomery may lie nearby. Fieldwalking of the area near the pits has led to the discovery of bloomery sites, and although it has not been possible to date these sites, continued brick clay extraction means that they will be regularly monitored.

A recent discovery, which has yet to be fully investigated, is that of ironworking slag associated with early medieval pottery in woodland south of Outwood, east of Horley in Surrey. The pottery has been identified as dating from the Saxo-Norman period, not later than about 1150. The Outwood area, hitherto regarded as of little interest archaeologically, has been attracting attention because evidence of a variety of periods has been coming to light. Not least of these is in connection with iron-making, and in the woodland where this early evidence of ironworking has come to light are the remains of similar workings tentatively dated by surface pottery finds to the thirteenth or fourteenth century. At present nothing is known of the ownership of this area in the eleventh or twelfth centuries.

By the thirteenth century documentary evidence suggests that iron production in the region had increased considerably. The Crown was purchasing iron from the Archbishop of Canterbury's estates in the Weald for several building projects, such as repairs to the castles at Guildford, in Surrey, and Leeds, in Kent (*colour plate 11*). In one order alone from 1242, 8000 horseshoes and 20,000 nails were ordered for delivery within a mere eight days! It seems unlikely that the Archbishop's estates had sufficient ironworks to complete such an order in such a short time, so it is reasonable to assume that the estate's agents were able to purchase the iron that was needed from ironworks all over the Weald, and perhaps beyond. Only a dozen sites can be positively dated to the thirteenth century, and for them to be able to produce iron in that sort of quantity seems inconceivable. Accounting for such output remains an important challenge for archaeologists and historians.

The documented purchases of iron, recorded in the rolls of the thirteenth and fourteenth century, serve to illustrate a number of different aspects of the iron industry in the Weald. Firstly, they acknowledge its existence and scale. The requirement, by the Crown, for nails and bars for building projects at the royal establishments, and for wedges, pegs, horseshoes and arrowheads for military purposes, as well as blooms for their own smiths to work up, shows that sufficient production capacity, often at short notice, was available in the region. All these orders were for several tons of iron at a time. If, as has been suggested, the Wealden bloom size was about 30lb, the 30,000 horseshoes requisitioned in 1254, weighing nearly 6½ tons, would have needed more than 1000 blooms – the annual output of six or seven bloomeries. One must presume that this was not the entire output of the industry at the time, and in any case the trade in iron was sufficient to encourage the imposition of a toll on its carriage through Lewes in the 1260s. What these orders also do is to set Wealden iron in this period in a national context, for even with construction works in the south-east, orders were being placed in Gloucester for iron from the Forest of Dean, the quality of which, compared with that from the Weald, was recognised generally as being in a higher league. There was also competition from imported Spanish iron which was arriving at south coast ports in this period.

There is little doubt that the latter part of the thirteenth century was a period of population increase in much of England, and that the spread of agriculture into marginal lands would have both stimulated the need for iron for farming implements, as well as generating additional employment for the inhabitants in crafts such as iron-making. Just such an area may have been Parrock, in Hartfield parish, where a cluster of ironworking sites has been identified, many of which also had a scatter of medieval pottery (*19*). Also identified was the site of a group of cottages where there was an abundance of pottery from the late twelfth to the early sixteenth centuries, as well as bloomery slag, nails and clay daub, suggesting that there had been a small settlement of ironworkers. The references to iron which appear from time to time in the High Weald are no great surprise. Purchases in Robertsbridge, Rotherfield

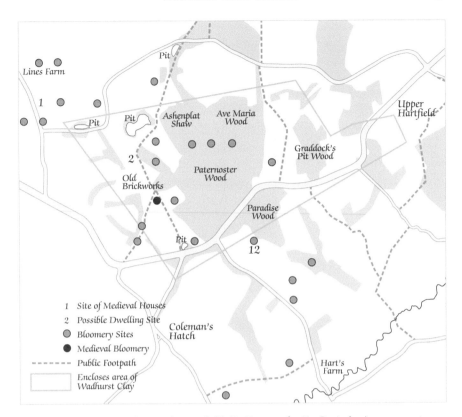

19 Bloomery sites around Parrock, Hartfield (*R. Bourne, after R. Cottingham*)

and Penshurst in the early fourteenth century, all for the repair of carts or ploughs, are contemporary with references to smiths in the Robertsbridge and Brightling areas. One in particular, the payment of a bloom of iron as a manorial due by Ralph Kenne of Dallington or Brightling, has come to light in the records of the Manor of Wartling in 1310. Kenne may have been related to one of the smiths in the Brightling area, where his family are known in the late thirteenth and early fourteenth centuries, and his works may well have been in operation for a couple of decades before the reference in question.

Other documentary mentions of purchases of iron have been noted in western Sussex, particularly in association with Petworth manor. However, this is an area where evidence of iron-making in the Middle Ages has been absent. Recent discoveries have, however, begun to reveal areas where production may have taken place. Chance finds of iron slag in association with medieval pottery have occurred at Southwater, south of Horsham, at Alfold, in Surrey, and most recently, at Loxwood, just to the south of Alfold, over the Sussex border. In some instances the finds have been linked to manorial remains and it seems very likely that the manor was the unit within which iron-making flourished during at least part of the Middle Ages. Further to the west, medieval pottery has been found in association with bloomery slag close to the edge of Ludshott Common, just over the Hampshire border.

In the majority of cases it is the sale of iron which figures most frequently in the records. Occasionally there are references to mining. An example is the dispute, in 1263, between Agnes Malameins and Isabel de Aldham over the profits of an iron mine near East Grinstead. The iron mine was part of the Lavertye estate which, two centuries earlier, may have included the *ferraria* mentioned in the Domesday Book. Another dispute concerning an iron mine involves damage being done to the public highway by John Neal and others, all of whom were probably mining the waste at Horley in Surrey. Discoveries at Outwood, mentioned earlier, have added to the interest in this area of the Surrey Low Weald. In addition to this example of iron mining and the occurrence of thirteenth- and fourteenth-century pottery in association with bloomery slag in Burstow parish, remains of ironworking at Thundersfield Castle, Horley, a moated site with pottery dating from the same date range, were excavated in the 1930s.

What appears to be a concentration of iron-making in the Horley/Outwood area in the thirteenth and fourteenth centuries, is paralleled by the discovery, in Crawley, just a few miles to the south, of similar activity in the same period and also in the following century. In the lists drawn up of people in Crawley liable to pay the Lay Subsidy, a property tax, in 1296, Gilbert the Blower had an obvious ironworking association, as did Reginald Smithson. Nearly a century later, residents eligible for the Poll Tax included William Rokenham and William Danecombe, each described as a *factor ferri*, or a maker of iron. Excavations in advance of the development of a new leisure complex at the north end of the town have uncovered large quantities of smelting and forging slag. Two hearths probably for the consolidation and forging of blooms, and an area of undoubted smithing debris, have also been found. Both hearths produced archaeomagnetic dates of around the turn of the fourteenth and fifteenth centuries, similar to the pottery found on the site, and nearly contemporary with the documented iron-makers. Other remains found in or near the High Street confirm that iron-making was of major importance in the town, which had been established early in the thirteenth century (*20*).

A few miles to the west of Crawley, Horsham is mentioned specifically in a number of the purchases by the Crown in the thirteenth and fourteenth centuries, and there seems little doubt that it was a centre of the production of arrows in the fourteenth century. The large ironworking site at Roffey, just east of the town, has yielded pottery from the thirteenth through to the fifteenth century, and a brief excavation in 1985 revealed the foundations of a building enclosing what appeared to have been a smithing hearth. A pond bay adjacent to the site suggests the possible use of water power at some stage. A number of late medieval buildings remain in the immediate area of the site,

20 Excavations of medieval ironworking at Kilnmead, Crawley, 1998 (*S. Stevens*)

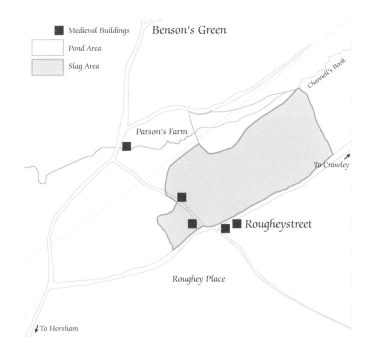

21 Roffey
medieval
bloomery site,
near Horsham
(*R. Bourne*)

perhaps indicating the existence of a relatively prosperous community at the time (*21*). Specific references in medieval documents to *la Rougheye* make this site one of particular importance for, while there exist no set of accounts for it, it remains the only ironworking location of the medieval Weald for which there is a reasonable certainty about the agreement of documentary and archaeological evidence.

Undoubtedly, full-scale excavation, which has not been attempted on any site of the period except Minepit Wood, would reveal much. It is increasingly clear that Crawley and Horsham constitute major concentrations of the iron industry in the late medieval period, and the continuing discoveries in the broad arc which stretches from south Surrey into central north Sussex, do seem to indicate an area where iron-making was of importance to a significant proportion of the population. The discovery of iron production in a medieval urban setting at Crawley may provide a clue to where other centres of iron-making existed in the Weald. So little excavation has taken place in Wealden towns and villages that the possibility must exist that some of them were similar centres of both smelting and forging. The occurrence of five people in Mayfield and four in Wadhurst all known as *faber*, or smith, in the late thirteenth century, as well as six smiths in Lindfield, near modern Haywards Heath, in the late fourteenth century, suggests such a possibility. All three places had a manorial connection with the Archbishop of Canterbury.

For evidence of the specific methods employed by iron-makers in the medieval Weald we have had to rely on the small amount of excavation and the very limited documentary accounts. Only discoveries at Minepit Wood, Rotherfield, close to the first-century site of the same name, at Crawley, and at a manorial site on the North Downs at Alsted, north of Merstham in Surrey, which had Wealden connections, have given us any information about medieval smelting technology. The accounts of the ironworks at Tudeley, which are examined in more detail below, offer some technical details, but of the type of the equipment used rather than the processes employed. As it is generally understood, the medieval iron-making process in the Weald was a limited development of that used by the Romans more than 1000 years earlier, and the evidence of the excavation in Minepit Wood and in Crawley shows that the smelting and other hearths were not much larger. In other respects the remains of sites from the Roman and medieval periods are similar. The identification of most medieval sites has been arrived at through pottery dating.

A continuing problem that exists with the identification of medieval sites is the suspicion that in many cases they continued in use into the post-medieval period and the evidence has disappeared beneath subsequent remains. To some extent this was confirmed at Chingley forge, near Lamberhurst, which was excavated prior to the construction of the Bewl Water. There, the remains of what was probably a fourteenth-century forge lay beneath two later, post-medieval phases of similar use. Although the interpretation of the earliest phase of the Chingley site as a forge is somewhat tentative on archaeological grounds, it is backed up by contemporary references to demesne ironworks on the estate of Boxley Abbey which included Chingley manor at that period. What is also of particular interest with Chingley is the use of water power, although there is no suggestion that it was anything other than a forge, or stringhearth. Bloomhearths, where water power assisted the smelting of iron, are known from other parts of the country, but their identification in the Weald has proved difficult. However, there is a small number of sites where evidence of both bloomery slags and the use of water power have led to the conclusion that they may have had just such a use (*22*). In some instances, such as Newbridge, near Hartfield, Brookland forge, near Frant, or Little Forge, at Buxted, the sites had subsequent use when the indirect blast furnace process was introduced. The majority are in eastern Sussex, although the only site to which a medieval context, without a later one, can be applied with any confidence, is the pond bay at Roffey, in north-west Sussex, mentioned above. Several forges are mentioned in deeds in the fifteenth century, particularly in the eastern Weald, around Ticehurst and Burwash, but their sites have so far eluded field walkers.

Accounts of ironworks in the medieval Weald are rare. Early in the fourteenth century the stock belonging to the forge of John de Lynleghe, at Withyham, was confiscated by the Crown, but the details are insubstantial. By far the most significant evidence of medieval ironworking practice lies in the accounts of the ironworks at Tudeley, in Kent, which belonged to Elizabeth de Burgh, the foundress of Clare College, Cambridge, and granddaughter of Edward I. They are the only accounts known of any ironworks in the Weald

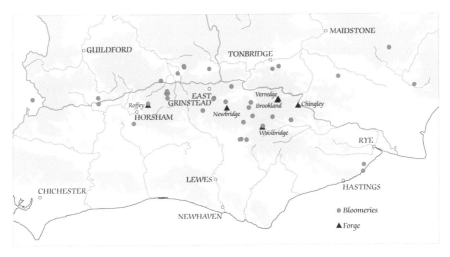

22 Medieval bloomery sites; triangles indicate the use of water power (*R. Bourne*)

in the medieval period, and provide a great deal of information about iron-making in the region in the fourteenth century. Lady de Burgh's estate at Southfrith, south-east of Tonbridge, had formed part of an extensive land holding in England, Wales and Ireland, which had been divided up in about 1317. The accounts, while being complete, do not include some aspects of production and trade which would have greatly assisted us in making sense of the industry generally. Housed in the National Archives, the detailed records of the ironworks survive for two periods – from 1329 to 1334 and from 1350 to 1354 – and refer to most of the stages in the production of raw iron, but do not include the forging of blooms, which was not, it seems, carried out at Tudeley. Inevitably the accounts provide us with the only case study of a medieval ironworks, but what little evidence there is from elsewhere does not contradict this use of the Tudeley material. The actual site of the ironworks has not been confidently located.

Essential to the iron-making process in any period is the acquisition of the raw materials. Wood was required in two forms: as charcoal for smelting, and as *elyngwood* for roasting the ore before smelting. The wood for charcoal was obtained initially by the *decena*, or ten, which contained 24 quarters (six hundredweight), but later by the *duodena* or dozen. A subdivision of a ten or a dozen is given as a sumpter, or pack-horse load, to which one assumes the ten or dozen also refers. It has been calculated that 100 blooms of iron required between 15 and 16 dozen (loads) of charcoal. There is no indication that wood was being coppiced, and there are occasional references to *olwood*, presumably old wood or fallen branches, being used. Wood was obtained, in general, from the Southfrith estate although some was clearly purchased from outside. In the three year lease granted in 1354 to Richard Colpeper, 50 dozen loads of charcoal were to be allowed to the lessee as well as 12 cartloads of *elyngwode*.

Iron ore was referred to in the accounts either simply as stone for making blooms, or specifically as *orston*, an English word for which no Latin equivalent seems to have existed at the time. The ore was quantified in hundreds according to the number of blooms which could be made from it. Because we do not know the size of a bloom we have no means of working out the ratio of ore to finished iron, except that the ratio is unlikely to have been markedly different from that found in the Roman period, about 10:1. Assuming an average weight of a bloom of about 10lb (4.5kg), then approximately 90lb (40kg) of ore would have been required for each bloom and more than 6¾ tons for a year's average annual production of 170 blooms, weighing 2¼ tons. Digging for ore was, like the cutting of wood, carried out on the estate, although no details are given of the methods used in digging, or of the nature of the excavations involved.

Frequent references in the accounts are made to repairs, to both equipment and buildings. From the itemised records of this work we can gain some idea of the technology being used, as well as being able to draw comparisons with the post-medieval period, for which inventories and accounts are more plentiful. No details are given of furnaces, but bellows and their maintenance, repair or replacement figure frequently. Maintenance usually involved the application of grease, presumably to keep the leather supple, although some sort of hinge may have been incorporated into the mechanism. In the eighteenth century, at Ashburnham furnace, greasing the bellows leather was an annual debit on the accounts. White leather, possibly deer hide, was used when the bellows needed more substantial repair, and in 1354 there was the expense of *brakyng*, or softening it. An ox hide had been purchased to cover the bellows during major refurbishment in 1350. Also used in bellows repair was hare skin, possibly for the valves. The tuyeres directed the air from the bellows into the furnace, and they were made of iron and purchased from a smith. The great heat to which they were subjected made it necessary for them to be replaced quite often. Other tools had to be purchased and maintained from time to time. Bellows grease was also used to lubricate and protect some metal tools, such as the hammers, tongs and axes that were needed. Axes were used for splitting blooms, and it has been suggested that this was to make the blooms into a more manageable size for smiths. However, the practice of cleaving blooms as a means of quality control has been observed in the very recent past among bloomery iron-makers in Sri Lanka and southern India. Splitting the bloom across half of its width, which took place while it was still hot, enabled the iron-maker to see a section of the iron, and ensure that the bloom had been properly consolidated. It also allowed the purchaser to see for himself that he was buying a sound bloom.

Other pieces of equipment which required purchase and repair were the various containers used to carry material about the works. A *scope*, or scoop, was employed, perhaps in measuring quantities of charcoal. Pairs of *coddes*, or bags, were also bought, although their purpose is unclear. In the eighteenth century, John Fuller, at Heathfield furnace, described the baskets, called *boshes*, which his fillers used for loading the charge of ore and charcoal into the furnace. *Treys*, or troughs, at Tudeley may have had the same purpose.

During the overall period covered by the accounts, the works underwent rebuilding in 1343 and substantial refurbishment in 1350. The accounts make it clear that the works included a building of about the size of a large shed, perhaps about 50m² of ground area. It was timber framed and had lath and daub walls, and a roof covered in wooden boards, a practice not uncommon in that period. The provision of a lock and key in the lease granted to Richard Colpeper in 1354 makes it clear that it would have been unoccupied for lengthy periods while expensive tools and equipment were stored inside. It is not apparent, though, whether the furnace was within the building as was suggested by the foundations of the building excavated at Minepit Wood, Rotherfield (*23*). A reconstruction of that building suggested a daub and wattle

23 Artist's reconstruction of the medieval bloomery site in Minepit Wood, Rotherfield
(*S. Howard, after S. Rigold*)

enclosure, with a thatched area at one end covering the bellows, and a roof and chimney above the furnace. At Tudeley the 425m of board purchased for the roof suggests a structure which was altogether different.

Of the manpower at the ironworks, references to named individuals are few. Generally the only skilled personnel mentioned were the blowers who, from 1350, we know were four in number: a master blower, named in 1354 as John Tubbe, and three other blowers. Working two at a time would mean that there was just one furnace, which corresponds well with the production of one bloom per day accounted for in the payments to the blowers, allowing for Sundays and other holy days. The importance of the blowers gives added significance to the name of Gilbert the Blower, one of the taxpayers of Crawley a few decades earlier. The only other worker mentioned is a contract stone digger. The other individuals referred to in the accounts were all estate staff or managers of the ironworks.

Of particular interest are the costs incurred by the ironworks (*24*). Each year's accounts contain both income and expenditure of generally similar elements. The income largely comprises the sale of blooms, although there are occasional references to other sales, such as dead wood being sold to the charcoal burners, and ore being sold by the estate when the works were let in 1333. An unusual sale was of *graynes* of iron, which, it has been suggested, may have been used to make steel. Apart from the *graynes* the bloom was the only product of the ironworks. Therefore the bulk of each season's accounts relates to expenditure, which fell into four main categories: the purchase of ore, the purchase of charcoal, the repair of tools and buildings, and the

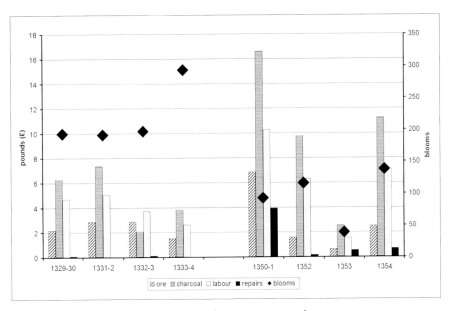

24 Tudeley ironworks expenditure and production 1329-34 and 1350-54

payment of the blowers. With the exception of one season, the highest proportion of expenditure was on the purchase and carriage of charcoal, which averaged 46 per cent of the money paid. The sale of wood in 1329-30 implied that, unlike in the post-medieval period, when ironmasters often contracted for coppice wood and then simply paid charcoal burners to make it into charcoal, the fuel costs at Tudeley included the cost of the green wood. An average of 17 per cent of costs were spent on ore, which included the digging, carriage and *elyng*, or burning. Richard Colpeper's 1354 lease of the works, as well as allowing him 50 dozen of charcoal, also let him have enough ore for 300 blooms, that is to say 100 blooms a year for 3 years, and 12 cartloads of *elyngwode*. There is no mention of workers at the works other than the blowers, and it is therefore possible that some or all of them were responsible for the payment of labourers who worked for them. Their wages accounted for an average of 34 per cent of the expenditure and included a piece-work payment for each bloom made and drink money which was, it states, according to the custom of the country. There was also a bonus paid according to status, the master blower receiving the largest amount and his subordinates proportionately less. Between 1331 and 1333 the workmen also received a seventh part of the output of the works, in blooms, from which they could derive some income on the open market, however this practice was short-lived. In addition, included in the payments to the personnel at the works in the 1350s were the wages of the keeper, and also the annual cost of a gown for him. While the proportions expended on ore, charcoal and labour charges remained fairly consistent throughout the periods of the accounts, repair and maintenance costs fluctuated.

The accounts survive from periods either side of the outbreak of the Black Death, and if one looks at individual amounts, as opposed to proportions of the overall charges, there are clear differences. To start with, there was the amount for which blooms were sold. In the 1330s these cost an average of 1s 4d each, rising to around 3s 5d in the 1350s; a rise of 256 per cent. Charcoal prices are a little harder to compare as the quantities in which they were delivered changed during the period of the accounts. Presumably, though, there was a direct relationship between the ten and the dozen, the two measurements used, which might account for a 20 per cent increase in any case. In the 1330s the price of charcoal averaged at 3s 7d a *decena* which, with a 20 per cent increase to bring it up to a *duodena*, would raise it to 4s 1½d. Twenty years later, though, in the years immediately following the pestilence, it stood at around 8s for each *duodena*; an increase of nearly 90 per cent. Ore digging does not seem to have suffered such a high inflationary increase, rising from around 19s for sufficient *oreston* to make 100 blooms, to about 26s, but it is the wages paid to the blowers that account most significantly for the high increase in the sale price of iron. In the pre-plague years the blowers, or fore-blowers, were paid at a rate equivalent to about 5d or 6d a bloom. This is because included in their payment was a seventh part of the production in blooms. Without this their pay came to about 2½d a bloom. That practice had been discontinued by the second period of accounts, so we must adjust the rates of pay to exclude this additional element if we are to be able to compare like with like before and after the Black Death. By the 1350s the rate of pay per bloom had risen to an average of 8d; an increase of 320 per cent. Carriage costs also increased, although comparisons are less easy because of inconsistencies in the methods used to itemise them in the accounts. Often the cost of ore and *elyng* wood are combined, and with the carriage of charcoal there is the disparity of the *decena* and the *duodena*. Nevertheless, where direct comparisons are possible the cost of carting ore can be seen to have increased by 150 per cent, while for charcoal it rose by as much as 200 per cent.

The orders being placed by the Crown in the thirteenth and fourteenth centuries implied high output by some ironworking sites. So far, only the sites at Roffey and probably Crawley look as though they were capable of such a level of production. Neither Tudeley nor Minepit Wood, where there was only one furnace, could have contributed significantly to such output, unless the number of sites of that scale was considerably greater than we know of at present. So far, 36 medieval ironworking sites have been identified in the Weald by archaeology, and with only 29 per cent of known bloomery sites dated to any particular period, there are likely to be many more as yet undated.

4

BLAST FURNACES AND FORGES

At the end of the fifteenth century a new method of making iron was introduced into the Weald. The introduction of the blast furnace and forge considerably increased the scale of iron-making, both in terms of the consumption of raw materials and the amount of iron produced. A much greater investment of money and labour was required than when iron was being made in bloomeries. Two distinct stages had to be undergone before pure, or wrought, iron was produced, and this technology is therefore known as the indirect process.

THE BLAST FURNACE

Blast furnaces had been in existence in parts of Europe since the twelfth century in Sweden and in Germany. They were probably being used in the Namur area in Belgium in the early part of the fifteenth century, and it is likely that ironworkers from there took the process to northern France in the 1450s, after the end of the Hundred Years' War. It was not until the late fifteenth century that the technology reached England.

Similar to a bloomery only in so far as the charcoal and iron ore were charged into the top of the furnace and air was pumped in to raise the temperature, the blast furnace differed in scale, in the way air was pumped in, and in the consequent temperature – up to 1500°C – which resulted in a different type of iron being produced. By the time the blast furnace was introduced into England, it had developed into a stone tower, roughly square in plan and about 6-7m high. Externally, the sides of the furnace were inclined slightly towards the top and, on adjacent sides of the furnace, there were two square arches: the blowing arch, where the bellows were situated and from which air was pumped into the furnace, and the casting arch, which gave access to the hearth from where the molten slag and metal could be tapped or run out of the furnace.

25 Hammer Pond, St Leonard's upper forge

Since the air required for the blast was delivered via water-powered bellows, furnaces in the Weald had to be built near streams. A typical site was a narrow valley, with a pond formed by constructing a dam or 'bay' as they were locally known, usually no more than 100m long, from one side of the valley to the other (25). The pond bay often formed a causeway across the valley. The height of furnaces meant that they needed to be built in locations where access to the top, for charging, would be relatively simple. To overcome this problem, furnaces were usually built near to a natural bank so that a wooden bridge could be erected to allow barrows of charcoal and ore to be wheeled across and their load delivered into the throat of the stack. The side of the valley or the pond bay itself could fulfil this role. The bay would have been breached in two places: firstly, a sluice would control the flow of water from the pond along a wooden channel, or launder, to the waterwheel; secondly, a spillway, probably located at the opposite end of the bay from the sluice, would allow water to overflow from the pond when the sluice was closed or there was a surplus of water because of heavy rain. Water and molten iron are a potentially explosive combination, so it was very important to ensure that water crossing an ironworking site was confined to specific channels. The spillway channel was often isolated from the working area of the site by an earthen bank. However, the water from the waterwheel had to pass close to the furnace; indeed, the founder needed to be able to control the flow of water to manage the blast of air from the bellows, so the tail race carrying the water would

26 Reconstruction of a Wealden blast furnace and gunfoundry (R. Houghton)

usually pass in front of the casting arch. For this reason, after passing over the waterwheel, the stream was generally culverted so that casting could take place safely above it. Once past the furnace and the working area, the tail race would rejoin the overflow stream (26).

There were two pairs of bellows, each about 5m long, and 750mm wide at the end furthest from the furnace. They were operated by a mechanism which was tripped by cams on a shaft, or axletree, rotated by a waterwheel about 4m in diameter. A counterbalance re-inflated the bellows between cam strokes which depressed the bellows alternately, allowing a continuous flow of air. The air from the bellows entered the furnace through a metal tuyere. It has been suggested that because the air came from two pairs of bellows, it needed to pass through a box which would balance the flow; however, there is insufficient evidence to confirm this in the Weald. The excavated remains of the bellows shaft at Chingley furnace, in Kent, showed that there were three sets of cams for each pair of bellows. Documentary evidence indicates that, between them, furnace bellows pumped about 12 times a minute on average, which would necessitate two rotations of the waterwheel. Furnaces had to be kept in blast as long as possible, so the bellows were operating 24 hours a day, stopping only for casting or to tap the slag. For this reason it was essential to ensure a reliable supply of water and, because of the relatively low rainfall in south-east England, it was often necessary to construct additional 'pen' ponds to act as storage reservoirs for the main furnace pond. Sometimes these ponds formed lengthy chains. The most considerable system known was the 30 ponds constructed to supply Iridge furnace, near Hurst Green, Sussex, in the sixteenth century (*colour plate 12*).

Internally the blast furnace resembled an upturned bottle, with the walls narrowing at a point known as the boshes, equivalent to the 'shoulders' of the bottle, to constrict the downward movement of the burning ore and charcoal, and allow molten iron and slag to drip into the hearth at the bottom of the furnace (27). The hearth was a stone-built bath, which rested on a heavy metal slab, and which sometimes protruded from the front of the furnace to allow easy access. As the molten metal accumulated in the hearth, the slag, which was less dense, floated on top of the iron, and periodically each was allowed to flow out of the furnace through holes in the front of the hearth. When cool, the slag was discarded on heaps, while the iron was run into channels and either solidified in open beds as lengths of iron called sows or pigs, or into pre-formed moulds to make castings. Smelting caused the gradual erosion of the walls of the hearth, which allowed for a progressively greater quantity of molten iron to be held in the furnace and for larger castings to be made, but it also increased the possibility of the iron breaking out of the furnace – a potentially dangerous event. Once the furnace had been blown out, a period of at least a month was needed for the hearth and the lower part of the internal stack to be rebuilt, before it could be blown in again.

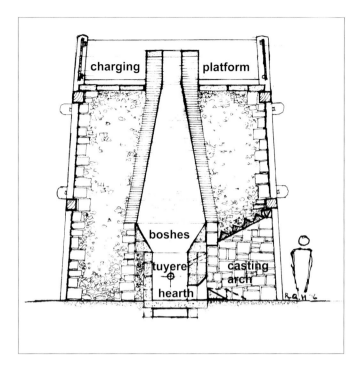

27 Blast furnace
elevation
(R. Houghton)

Blast furnaces were usually 'blown in' after the harvest, in about October, and the smelting period, known as a campaign, continued until late spring, when the diminishing rainfall caused the supply of water to lessen. Founders would have to proceed carefully at the beginning of a blast, getting the furnace up to heat and allowing the internal walls of the stack to become vitrified and resistant to the corrosive effect of the iron. Iron cast in the first few weeks would be of inferior quality. It was necessary at all stages of a campaign to keep the state of the furnace under constant supervision. Changes in temperature could affect the efficiency of the smelting process, and deteriorating air supply was often the cause of a lower temperature and a consequent build-up of partially smelted material on the inside of the stack. The tuyere needed to be regularly kept clear to prevent such problems. The founder was able to see into the furnace through an aperture, known as the 'founder's eye'; monitoring of the state of the chemical reaction taking place within the furnace was entirely dependant on observation of the colour, sound and movement of the combustion. The conditions within the furnace could be changed by altering the speed of the waterwheel, or by varying the proportions of the charcoal and iron ore in the charge. Tapping the iron from the hearth would occur once or twice a day, depending on what was being cast. A blast furnace could produce, on average, about a ton of iron a day. That amount varied, of course, with the size of the furnace; ones built in the first half of the sixteenth century having smaller capacities than those built nearly two centuries later. The daily output of a furnace also increased during the course of a campaign. Occasionally it was possible for furnaces to continue in blast for longer than the normal seven or eight months; in the early 1740s the furnace at Lamberhurst, which was fed from the River Teise, went for more than three years before being 'blown out', with the next campaign lasting nearly two years.

Around blast furnaces would have been a collection of buildings (*colour plate 13*). The bellows were housed in the blowing house, which protected them against the elements. Being made of leather, they were subject to rapid deterioration without such protection. Maintenance, such as greasing them to keep them supple, was carried out regularly. Over the casting area was another building, which served several purposes. Firstly it, too, protected the casting arch and the work going on there from the elements; a downpour of rain just when casting was taking place could be potentially dangerous in the open air. Secondly, because the founder needed to closely monitor the state of the iron in the hearth, which he could only do by observing its colour and listening to the sound of the air being forced in by the bellows, he needed a dark environment in which to work. Finally, the timber frame of the casting house provided a convenient structure for hoisting large castings, such as sows and cannon, in and out of wagons. Other buildings on furnace sites included sheds for the storage of ore and charcoal, and, in some cases, moulding shops where moulds for castings could be assembled. The map made in 1743 of the site of Cowden furnace shows just such a group of buildings (*colour plate 14*). As a gunfoundry it also had a boring house on site, as did Scarlets and Heathfield furnaces, among others, where the waste from cannon boring can still be found (*colour plate 15*). The buildings around ironworks were not infrequently used as shelters by vagrants. References in evidence given at Quarter Sessions hearings reveal instances of people at the bottom end of the social hierarchy probably finding warmth and a lack of prejudice there. Occasional entries in parish registers recording the burial of unnamed individuals, often children 'at the furnace' or 'at the hammer', can also be found.

Compared to furnaces built in other parts of Britain, Wealden ones were relatively small. The furnace stack at Panningridge, near Dallington, which was built in the 1540s, was a mere 5m square at the base. As time went on, furnaces were built larger. Maynard's Gate furnace, near Crowborough, which was built nearly 20 years later, was 6.5m square, and Pippingford furnace, at Ashdown Forest, built in the 1690s, one of the last in the Weald, was 7m square. The larger furnaces were at the base, the taller they were. We have no precise measurements of the heights of individual furnaces, none of the structures having survived. However, Emanuel Swedenborg, a Swedish writer on the iron industry, noted in 1734 that the furnace at Lamberhurst was 28ft (8.5m) high, the highest in the region. The generally small size of the earlier blast furnaces built in the Weald meant that large castings were difficult to make because of the limited amount of iron available in the hearth at any one time. To overcome this, two instances are known of double furnaces being built. The first was at Worth, which was built in 1546 by the Crown, almost certainly for the casting of large guns. The second was noted in 1574, and can probably be identified as Shillinglee furnace in western Sussex. The specific purpose of the double furnace there is not known.

FINERY FORGES

The higher temperature in the blast furnace resulted in the iron produced being different to that made in the bloomery. During smelting in the blast furnace, the iron absorbed some of the carbon from the charcoal, which altered the character of the metal. Whereas blooms of iron from a bloomery could be worked into bars or billets without further treatment, the cast iron from the blast furnace was brittle when cold, and had to undergo a secondary process to remove the carbon. This process was called fining and was carried out in a separate iron mill called a finery. Since it was developed in the southern part of Belgium, this method of forging cast iron into wrought iron is called the Walloon process.

The greatest demand for iron was for fashioning into tools, nails, wire and innumerable other objects, principally by blacksmiths, so the production of wrought iron bars, from which such things could be made, was the primary role of most Wealden ironworks. For this to be achieved, the basic product of the blast furnace was raw cast iron in the form of a sow or pig (28). Molten cast iron run from the hearth of a blast furnace into a shallow sand trough will form a beam of iron triangular or semi-circular in section. These were of no standard length – an example at Westfield is 3.4m long (colour plate 16). Early furnaces would be able to cast a single sow, which might weigh as much as half a ton, at each tapping of the hearth, but such pieces of iron were unwieldy and it was not uncommon for smaller ingots of iron, called pigs, to be cast instead of, or even in addition to, sows. Once cooled, a sow or pig cast at the furnace was brought to the finery and, a section at a time, gradually remelted in a hearth lined with iron plates, over a bed of charcoal under a blast of air (29). As the sow melted, the carbon was reduced and the iron formed a mass, also called a bloom, at the bottom of the hearth, which was then lifted out while still red hot and hammered to expel any slag. This process might be repeated until the finer judged, probably by the amount of heat required to melt it, that the amount of carbon in the iron was reduced from about 4 per cent down to about 0.1 per cent. No such scientific calculation was, of course, possible; the judgement was dependent on the finer's skill and experience. The mass of wrought iron that it had become, and which at this stage was known as a loop, was then transferred to a second hearth, called the chafery, which more closely resembled a large blacksmith's hearth. There it was slowly

Vol. IV, Forges, 2ᵉ Section, Pl. IX.

28 Casting sows (*from Diderot & Alembert, Encyclopédie, 1751-72*)

29 Cast-iron pig from St Leonard's lower forge, one end partly drawn off in the finery (scale 10cm)

formed into a bar. Using a heavy, water-powered hammer, the hammerman, the other skilled artisan working at the forge, would first form the loop into a rough block (*30*). Then working from the middle of the loop, and frequently returning it to the chafery hearth to be brought back up to sufficient heat,

Right: 30 Forge hammer head from Etchingham
forge; Anne of Cleves House Museum, Lewes

Below: 31 Forging wrought-iron bars (*from
Diderot & Alembert, Encyclopédie, 1751-72*)

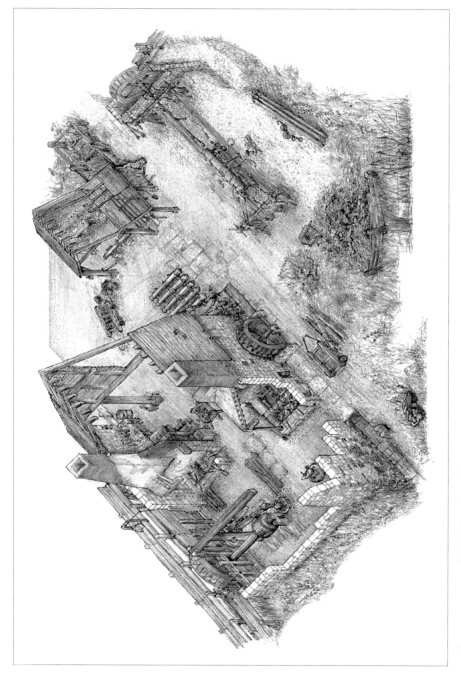

32 Reconstruction of a Wealden finery forge and boring mill (*R. Houghton*)

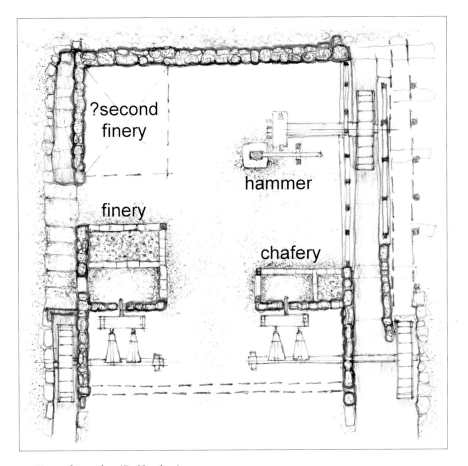

33 Finery forge plan (*R. Houghton*)

he would move it under the great hammer to gradually work it, first into an ancony, a mass of iron with a narrow waist and bulbous ends, and then finally into a bar, about 3m long, the form in which it would be sold (*31*).

Finery forges, which are also known as Hammers, and memorably in place names such as Abinger Hammer and the hamlet of Hammer, near Haslemere, were housed in rectangular buildings (*32*). They were generally about 10m wide, with the hammer and chafery along one side and the finery (sometimes there were two of these) along the other (*33*). The hammer, and the bellows for each of the hearths, all needed a water supply and a water-wheel mechanism. Thus a forge might need as many as four waterwheels. Like the furnace, the forge would have a pond, often known as the hammer pond, but instead of the two breaches in the pond bay, there would need to be at least three: the overflow spillway, and up to four sluices, two each side of the forge building. The management of the flow of water from these sluices was complicated by the fact that the waterwheels would be in close proximity and, because of the need to position the hearths and hammer inside the building in such a way as to make it easy to manoeuvre hot and heavy metal between them. The waterwheels on the same side of the building would probably rotate in opposite directions. This necessitated letting the water flow onto each wheel in such a way as to avoid water backing up from one wheel to another. The usual method was to offset the wheel races (the wood-lined channels in which the wheels rotated). Unlike the furnace, which was required to be in blast all day, every day, for several months at a time, forge operation was intermittent. Although it would have been unlikely for all the wheels to be in use at once, the demand for water for a forge could be greater than for a furnace at certain times. Since such a potentially heavy demand could restrict the flow of water downstream of a forge, furnaces were usually located upstream from forges or in separate valleys. In a number of instances forges and furnaces occupied the same site, examples include Riverhall, near Wadhurst, and Burningfold, near Dunsfold. In none of the examples known, though, is there enough evidence to suggest that both operations were being carried on at the same time. In

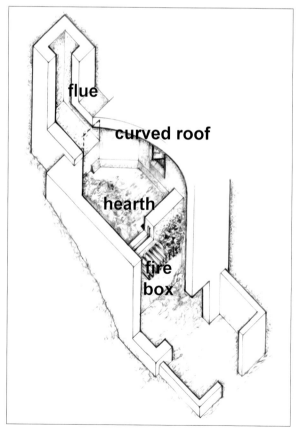

34 Reconstruction of an air, or reverberatory, furnace (*R. Houghton*)

some instances, such as at Langleys, in Maresfield, the two operations were separated by a considerable interval of time.

Although common in other parts of England, forges with two finery hearths were relatively uncommon in the Weald. Only three sites of forges have been excavated: at Chingley, near Goudhurst, at Ardingly and at Blackwater Green, near Crawley; the first two appear to have had only one finery hearth. However, the discovery of offset wheel pits at Blackwater forge suggests the possibility of four waterwheels and therefore a second finery. The small illustration of the mill building at Langleys forge, Maresfield, on a mid seventeenth-century map, shows three chimneys, which also indicates the presence of a second finery hearth (*colour plate 17*) and correspondence preceding the lease of Robertsbridge forge to John Churchill in 1754 reveals that Churchill intended reinstating the second finery hearth that William and George Jukes, his predecessors at the works, had converted into an air furnace. This second finery had been part of the original forge built in 1541.

Due to the more conventional layout of a forge (compared to a furnace), conversion of forge buildings to other mill uses once their original purpose was finished, such as fulling woollen cloth or grinding corn, was not uncommon. Simply by the removal of the hammer mechanism, which was largely held together by wedges, and the demolition of the hearths, the building could be emptied and new machinery installed. Other reuses included paper making, as at Bramshott Hammer, and silk crepe making as at Thursley. The conversion of Woodcock Hammer, near Lingfield, to a wire mill was not related to its earlier use as a finery. Instead the metal used was imported from outside the Weald.

AIR FURNACES

Air furnaces were used for remelting metal for casting into moulds (*34*). Sometimes known as reverberatory furnaces, they relied on the up-draught from a tall chimney to generate sufficient heat to melt the metal. They were principally used in urban locations, where there was no water supply to power bellows, and most often for non-ferrous metals like copper and bronze. Use of such furnaces is known, or is implied, in a few instances in the Weald. The example mentioned above at Robertsbridge may have been for casting cannon balls, which were much in demand during war time. Another air furnace recorded as being built during the same period is the one at Hamsell furnace, near Rotherfield, which was built for the executors of William Harrison in 1745. On a number of occasions they purchased 'melting iron', that is pre-smelted iron, for making into products that did not have to be made directly from ore, such as shot or wheels for gun carriages. A small number of Wealden founders branched out into casting guns in bronze. John Browne diversified in this way during the 1630s when there was a disinclination by the navy to purchase iron cannon. He set up a foundry at his works at Brenchley, in Kent, which must have included an air furnace. Over a century later there is some evidence to suggest that William Bowen was casting guns in bronze at one of his furnaces – Barden, near Tonbridge, or Cowden – in the 1750s, necessitating the installation of an air furnace. A decade later Edward Raby offered to cast bronze mortars for the Board of Ordnance, the government department responsible for purchasing for the army and navy. A small splash of gunmetal found at Warren furnace, his works near East Grinstead, tentatively indicates that he may have had an air furnace there.

STEEL–MAKING

Steel was recognised for its toughness during the Middle Ages, and high-quality metal from Spain and the Middle East was imported for specialist weapons. The Germans, in particular those from the Sauerland, to the east of the Rhine valley, were also skilled steel-makers. Steel-making in the Weald dates from the early sixteenth century, but it was never an important product of the region. Its production was based on a modification of the finery process. Steel contains between about 0.1 and 2.0 per cent carbon, whereas cast iron may contain up to around 4 per cent carbon. Wrought iron contains the least amount of carbon, it being the aim of finers to eliminate carbon completely and achieve an iron equivalent to that produced in a bloomery. In steel-making, the skill is to partially decarburise cast iron, that is to reduce the amount of carbon in the iron to the extent that it takes on the distinctive properties of steel. That was easier said than done, so it may have been more effective to put the cast iron through the finery process to make wrought iron, and then re-carburise it by the deliberate addition of carbon, in the form of charcoal, or other organic material. Later steel-making processes, such as cementation and crucible steel, used in other parts of Britain, involved variations on that method. A steel forge was built on Ashdown Forest as early as about 1505, a short distance upstream from Newbridge furnace, but appears to have stopped working by 1539. The Sidney family were probably the Weald's most important steel producers, having mills at Robertsbridge forge and at an as yet unidentified site at Boxhurst, near Sandhurst in Kent. They employed German workmen, but competition from Germany caused the venture to be short-lived. A later steel forge existed in Warbleton, Sussex, in the seventeenth century, although no details of its specialist operation are known.

5

IRON PRODUCTION IN THE SIXTEENTH TO NINETEENTH CENTURIES

The first known blast furnace in the Weald, and most likely in Britain, was in operation by the end of 1490 at Buxted in Sussex. The furnace, and probably forge, at Queenstock were being worked on land belonging to the Archbishop of Canterbury, whose estates had supplied considerable quantities of iron to the Crown a couple of centuries earlier. We know nothing about who it was being operated by, what was being made there, where its raw materials were coming from or its products going to. In less than 20 years, however, the ironworks were being referred to in the past tense, the pond being empty, only for it to be revived a few years later and subsequently go on to play a significant role in the 1540s, remaining in operation for a further 20 years or more. The setting up of Queenstock was followed, some six years later, by another blast furnace, which was constructed as a result of a commission, by Henry VII, at Newbridge, in Hartfield parish on Ashdown Forest. In fact, a furnace there had been planned five years earlier, when the king was considering a military intervention against the French in support of the Duchy of Brittany. In the event, it was war against the Scots which prompted the building of the ironworks for the production of heavy metalwork for gun carriages.

Unlike the furnace at Queenstock, the works at Newbridge, which belonged to the Crown, are well documented. Setting up the works was placed in the hands of a goldsmith based in Southwark, called Henry Fyner. Having set them up, he did not operate the works himself, but leased them to Peter Roberts, or Graunt Pierre as he was known, a French ironworker. The lease, which was for eight years, included the right to take wood and ore from the forest, then part of the estates of the Duchy of Lancaster. Fyner rejoined the operation after a few months and acted as distributor for the iron produced there, but the tenancy came to an abrupt end after only two years when Roberts got into financial difficulties and was imprisoned. The new tenant, Pauncelett Symart, also French, did not fare much better, but he managed to retain the lease of the works for the next 14 years. The product range was

35 Stumblets furnace bay, Maresfield

extended and cast guns with detachable chambers were produced. Seemingly an innovation, the continued use of wrought iron weapons suggests they were not a success. The Crown's continued involvement with the Newbridge furnace is emphasised by the works being leased to Humphrey Walker, the King's gunfounder, in 1512. Sir Thomas Boleyn, father of the future queen, became the occupier in 1525. Being one of the earliest furnaces built in the Weald, it was likely to have been of small capacity and output, and in 1539 the Crown built a replacement a few miles to the west, on the edge of Ashdown Forest at Stumblets (35). Newbridge continued working in private hands until the end of the century. Meanwhile, other ironworks were being set up. These included the steel forge a short distance upstream from Newbridge, in about 1505, and a furnace and forge at Parrock, in Hartfield in 1513.

At Newbridge much of the skilled work was in the hands of immigrant ironworkers from France, and during the first 40 years of the sixteenth century a considerable number of founders, finers and hammermen migrated to the Weald. They brought with them skills learned in operating furnaces and forges on the other side of the English Channel. The economic circumstances which drove them to emigrate included a lack of investment in ironworking there, and the rising price of wood. In contrast to the situation in France, investment in the iron industry in the Weald was growing rapidly in the first half of the sixteenth century, so the migrant workers were able to find employment with relative ease, and it was not long before most communities in the Weald included French families. Nevertheless, the migrants may have taken a considerable time to integrate fully, keeping to themselves near to the ironworks with which they were most familiar. As is often the case with immigrants, the skilled workers were the first to move to England, their families following them later. First-generation immigration reached its peak in the 1520s; thereafter, the families intermarried, or married into the local population. Subsequent generations often continued in the iron trade, some rising to become ironmasters themselves. The immigrant workers came mainly from the Pays de Bray, which is a geologically similar region to the Weald, although smaller, lying inland from Dieppe in north-eastern Normandy (*36*). Blast furnaces and forges had been in operation there from after the 1450s, when ironworkers moved into the area from Jausse les Ferons, near Namur, in present-day Belgium. To be able to live in England, migrants had to show they were working for a native employer. Lists of the workers were drawn up showing who they were working for, where they had come from and, in some cases, when they had arrived in England. From these 'denization' lists it has

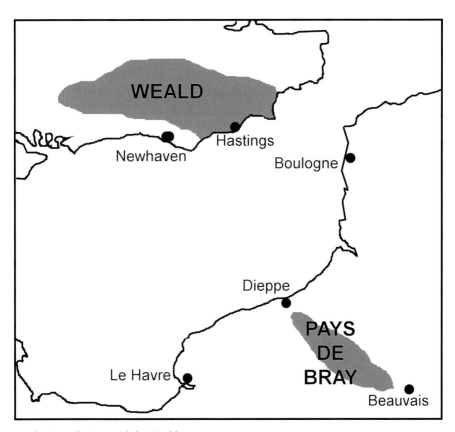

36 The Pays de Bray and the Weald

been possible to discover at which ironworks in France many of the migrant workers had been employed. Due to those compiling the lists being unfamiliar with the language, the workers' names were often transcribed phonetically, or anglicised, resulting in many of the names being changed.

The introduction of the new technology was very much in the hands of the major estates of the realm – the Church and the Crown. However, it was not long before other landowners began to see the potential for iron production in their own properties. Many of the sites that started in the 1520s were forges, some possibly still working up iron produced in bloomeries. Socknersh furnace, at Brightling, was in blast in the 1530s; John Collins, its ironmaster, being commemorated on the Weald's first cast-iron memorial in Burwash church. The religious and political events of the 1530s, which centred around the King's divorce from Catherine of Aragon and the break from the church in Rome, led to a build-up in the defensive capabilities of the kingdom, and the Dissolution of the Monasteries and smaller religious houses. Henry VIII had long taken a keen interest in armaments and had brought foreign gunfounders to London to cast bronze ordnance for his army and navy. The threat posed by the European powers, encouraged by the Pope, required a swift defensive response, but bronze weaponry was expensive. Iron guns, made by assembling bars and hoops of wrought iron, were also expensive and neither accurate nor reliable. Could the newly developing iron industry in Sussex be utilised to cast iron cannon instead? The process had been tried on the continent, but with limited success. William Levett, the rector of Buxted, was Deputy Receiver of the King's Revenues in Sussex and had taken control of the furnaces and forges operated by his late brother, John. Under Levett's management the skills of a local iron founder, Ralph Hogge, and of Peter Baude, a successful French founder of bronze guns, were brought together to produce a complete cast-iron cannon at Buxted in 1543 (37). Although only used for land defence at this time, the production of cast-iron cannon began in earnest, with Levett appointed the King's 'gunstonemaker'. Soon, a small number of other founders, such as Arthur Middleton, at Huggett's furnace, and Robert Hodson, at Pounsley, began to see it as a profitable trade. Levett himself needed to expand to meet demand, and was casting guns at the double furnace in Worth Forest.

In the 1540s gunfounding was the preserve of a select few ironmasters; most furnaces were engaged in the production of sows, for fining at forges into bar iron, which was sold to merchants and ironmongers both locally and further afield. Iron was carried up to London and shipped around the coast to ports for carriage to other regions. By 1548 there were 50 furnaces and forges at work in the Weald. Despite the complaints about their voracious consumption of wood, the number of furnaces and forges continued to grow. The other effect of the political and religious turmoil towards the end of Henry VIII's reign was the closure of the religious houses. Unlike in other parts of England, the monasteries in the South East had not been significantly

37 Peter Baude/Bowd's name on a bronze gun made for Henry VIII

involved in the iron industry. However, the dissolution of Robertsbridge Abbey in 1538 opened up an opportunity that Sir William Sidney seized when he purchased the site and demesne of the abbey in the following year. Within two years, work had started on the construction of a furnace and forge at Robertsbridge, and in 1542 land was obtained from the vicar of Penhurst for a second furnace, eight miles away on the edge of Panningridge Wood, north of Ashburnham. Having purchased a sizeable estate, it is somewhat surprising that Sir William leased additional land for the Panningridge furnace, but the demand for fuel in particular, for the two sites at Robertsbridge meant that the woodland on the estate needed to be reserved for them. While a second furnace would ensure that full advantage was taken of the capacity of the forge and its two fineries, it was necessary to locate it where there was ample woodland to sustain it. The building work and the subsequent operation of both of these sites was the subject of detailed accounts kept by the clerks of the ironworks, and comprises some of the best information we have about the operation of ironworks in this period. From the outset the new venture needed skilled supervision, and among those brought in to provide expertise were members of the Collins family who had established Socknersh furnace. Also, the founder for Panningridge furnace came from Buxted, several miles to the west, where there was already a skilled workforce.

The building accounts list the work of the masons and carpenters who erected the walls and wooden frameworks of the furnaces and the water channels. Also, work had to be done to cut down the trees and bushes where the pond was to be made, and assemble the bellows and their mechanisms. Once the ironworks were built, the accounts record the expenditure on raw materials, maintenance and the skilled workforce. Income was derived from the sale of iron from the forge to smiths, some agricultural produce, and beer for the workmen. Iron for the construction of Camber Castle was purchased from Robertsbridge. The furnace there ceased working in 1546, but Panningridge furnace continued to supply the forge with sows until 1563, by which time other furnaces in the neighbourhood, such as Socknersh, Netherfield and Mountfield, were also supplying the forge. Panningridge was subsequently let to a succession of tenants and continued in operation until the 1580s.

Sir William Sidney died in 1553 and the estate was taken over by his son, Henry (*colour plate 18*). In 1566 he embarked on a new venture, the setting up of steelworks at Robertsbridge and at Boxhurst, near Sandhurst, and the lease of a furnace and forge in Glamorgan, South Wales, from which iron was shipped to Robertsbridge. Steelworkers, described in the accounts as 'Dutchmen', were brought from the Sauerland in Germany. Initially a success, with steel being sold in London and other parts of southern England, the works gradually lost their market advantage to imports from the Baltic. Sir Henry Sidney gave up control of the Robertsbridge ironworks in 1573, leasing them to Michael Weston, an ironmaster who was to operate works as far apart as Cowden and Brede during the next few years.

The following year was to see an important milestone in the expansion of the iron industry in the Weald. The growth of gunfounding among a relatively small number of founders and the considerable success they achieved in the quality of their products, led to a growing demand for guns by foreign states. The government of Queen Elizabeth I were understandably concerned that they should be able to exercise control over the export of ordnance, and the queen's gunfounder, Ralph Hogge, who had played a pivotal role in casting the first iron cannon 30 years earlier, had been granted the sole right to cast guns for them. A complaint about this state of affairs was put before the Privy Council, which ordered that a list be drawn up of all the ironworks in the Weald, and that the ironmasters be obliged to enter into an agreement not to cast guns except with the permission of the Council, in breach of which it would cost them £2000; equivalent to over £300,000 in the early twenty-first century. In February of 1574 a messenger was dispatched to visit all the ironworks and obtain the compliance of the ironmasters. In the space of two weeks he had completed his task, and the lists compiled as a consequence provide us with a remarkable record of the state of the industry (*38*). No less than 50 furnaces and an equivalent number of forges

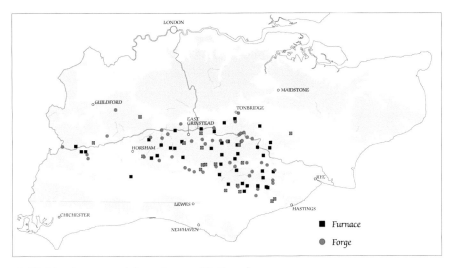

38 Wealden furnaces and forges in 1574 (*R. Bourne*)

were included in the lists, which were compiled in several versions. One list recorded the names of the landowners, another the number of ironworks in each parish. A third elaborated on the list of owners by commenting on which ironworks they owned, which other ones they occupied or who their tenants were. The lists complement, and occasionally contradict, each other, but are an invaluable source for historians. In several instances the 1574 lists are the first record we have of some ironworks; in a few cases, the lists are the only evidence we have. What is clear from the lists is that from the modest start at the beginning of the sixteenth century, and the impressive growth to 1548 when there were 50 ironworks, the number had doubled in a mere 25 years. That growth had, of course, a geographical dimension. From its early heartland around Ashdown Forest, ironworks had been established across the High Weald, into Kent and Surrey, and latterly on the far western margins of the region, close to the Hampshire border. What is also evident is the diversity of individuals involved in the iron industry. In the early days, it was the Crown, the Archbishop of Canterbury and the Duke of Norfolk who provided the financial impetus. Three-quarters of a century later, the Crown still owned Newbridge, and the works in St Leonard's Forest, near Horsham, but let them both. Lords Montague, Abergavenny and Buckhurst likewise handed over the furnaces and forges on their lands to a growing number of men whose principal occupation was making iron. Landowners like Sir Richard Baker and Sir Alexander Culpeper in Kent, or Sir Thomas Gresham and Sir Henry Sidney in Sussex took the rents from their estates made profitable by the ironworks other people worked, while otherwise engaged as courtiers or office holders. The majority of those who directly controlled the industry were the local gentry and yeomanry. The wealth they could make from iron enhanced their modest properties and enabled them to rebuild their houses and extend their influence. Some, like John Duffield of East Grinstead, who had ironworks near his home, but also co-owned works in Kirdford and Cranleigh, or Thomas Glyde, who occupied furnaces and forges in Etchingham, Mountfield and Herstmonceux, had almost become professional ironmasters. Some of the names that appear in the lists, like John Collins, then 80 years old, and Arthur Middleton, had been in the business for as long as 40 years; a few, such as John Lambard, who ran the Vachery forge at Cranleigh, were of immigrant stock.

At the centre of this stands the figure of Ralph Hogge. When William Levett died in 1554, he left his 'servant', Hogge, £10 and an amount of iron; not a large bequest even by the standards of the day. The term 'servant' meant Hogge was employed by Levett, and the nature of his involvement in the casting of the first successful iron cannon suggests that Hogge was Levett's assistant at Buxted. He was Levett's natural successor and probably continued to manage his late master's furnace. In 1559, in succession to Levett, he was appointed the Queen's 'gonnestonemaker' for life, and was married the following year to Margaret, the daughter of Edmund Henslowe, the master of game on Ashdown Forest. His newly acquired position enabled Hogge to set up two new furnaces, probably those at Marshalls and Langleys, in Maresfield, which he ran in conjunction with the Buxted furnace he had taken over from Levett, and Hendall furnace, which he must have leased from Nicholas Pope. All feature in the accounts which have survived for the years 1576-81, although some figure more frequently than others, the records being only a part of a larger body of material, the rest of which has been lost. The account book was kept by John Henslowe, Ralph Hogge's brother-in-law, who was clerk of the ironworks. The book was later reused by Henslowe's brother, Philip, an Elizabethan theatre owner.

Operation of Hogge's furnaces was similar in many ways to those of Sir William Sidney. However, Hogge was a gunfounder, so much of his production was geared towards the casting of ordnance and shot. Cast-iron sows were produced, especially at the start of a campaign when the quality of the iron in the hearth was not fine enough for casting into guns, although it is not clear if Hogge had a forge to which his sows could be sent. It is likely that the limited production of cast iron for fining did not make operating a forge viable. Of particular interest are the names of the individuals to whom guns and shot were being supplied. From 1568 Hogge had a licence to sell guns that were not required by the Crown. This allowed him to maintain production, which would have been difficult if his only market was the limited requirements of the government. Hogge was able to sell guns through a Mr Harman, of Lewes, who was probably supplying private shipping. Ralph Hogge's brother, Brian, is mentioned in the accounts. He held a post at the Tower of London, eventually being a Gunner. By 1581, when the accounts end, Ralph Hogge

39 The hog rebus on Hogge House, Buxted

had been in the iron business for 40 years. With the profits of his trade he built a house at Buxted, which bears his name to this day, and into the wall of which he set an iron plate cast with a hog (*39*). He died, lame and unlettered, in 1585, and was buried at the parish church.

The increasing tension between England and Spain and the growing prosperity of the kingdom served to increase the markets for iron in the 1580s, both domestically and overseas. However, from the 1550s furnaces and forges had begun to be built in other parts of England and Wales. This did not lessen the market for Wealden iron, much of which was directed towards London and the south and east coasts, which were largely removed from the areas of the country where new ironworks were being built. Indeed, furnaces and forges continued to be established in the Weald. Beckley furnace, set up in 1587, took advantage of easy access along the River Tillingham to the sea at Rye, which was to prove invaluable a century or more later. In the west, the iron ore in the Vale of Fernhurst attracted several ironmasters, with Coombe furnace in Rogate working in tandem with Habin forge, the latter making use of the good water supply issuing from the Greensand.

A brisk business in guns preceded the Armada scare in 1588, only to be followed by an attempt by the government to clamp down on their export once the threat had subsided. A new list of ironworks was ordered, using the lists of 1574 as a starting point, but only the part covering the county of Kent has survived. Nine furnaces and four forges were listed, and of the furnaces five specialised in casting guns (*40*). Instead of a number of lists recording similar, but slightly differing information, the list of 1588 is more succinct. From it we learn, for example, that Thomas Brattle owned Horsmonden furnace, but that

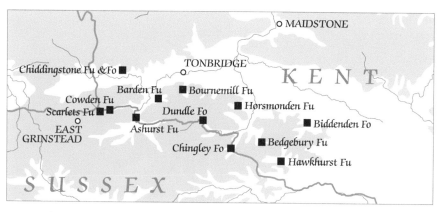

40 Kent furnaces and forges in 1588 (R. Bourne)

he had let it for many years to William Ashburnham. Ashburnham, in turn had let the furnace to Thomas Johnson (who had earlier worked for Ralph Hogge). Despite his apparently English-sounding name, Johnson may have descended from a family of immigrant ironworkers, for a succession of family members, starting with a Cornelius Johnson, had careers in gunfounding going back to the reign of Henry VIII. His kinsman, Francis Johnson also appeared in the Kent list, casting guns at Cowden furnace for John Swaysland. What we also learn from the list is that 68 minions and 46 falcons, guns cast at Horsmonden, had recently been taken, presumably along the River Medway, to Maidstone for onward transport to the Tower of London, and that some were, even then, waiting at Yalding and Maidstone for a vessel to take them on. Furthermore, the list even gives the name of the clerk of the furnace, Lewis Hughes. The number of furnaces and forges in Kent was small in comparison to those in Sussex in the same period, so it is a great regret that the 1588 list for Sussex, in particular, has not survived.

Another of the ironmasters mentioned in the 1588 list is Thomas Browne; at that time casting guns at Bough Beech furnace, near Chiddingstone, which he purchased from Thomas Willoughbie the following year. In 1596 Browne was appointed royal gunfounder and, like Ralph Hogge had before him, was able to consolidate his position by acquiring more furnaces: Ashurst in 1599 and Horsmonden in 1604. Browne and his fellow gunfounders came under increasing pressure from the government in the years leading up to the end of the sixteenth century. A series of measures were introduced to restrict the export of guns to the continent, including limiting the number of furnaces permitted to cast guns. It was made a requirement that all guns had to be sent to the Tower of London, and ship owners and masters were obliged to seek licences to export guns, preventing foreign vessels from engaging in the trade. Enforcement of these measures was not thorough, nor was adherence rigid.

The main strength in the Wealden iron industry continued to lie in the production of bar iron. Recent estimates have shown that output from the region grew slowly until the 1530s, after which the rate of growth began to climb steeply, reaching a peak in the early 1590s, when over 9000 tons were being produced a year. However, once furnaces and forges had begun to be established in other parts of England and Wales, production began to grow there equally rapidly, albeit some 30 years behind the Weald. As output in the rest of the kingdom increased, it was inevitable that some effect would be felt in the markets for Wealden bar iron. The drop in production that ushered in the new century was followed, at the end of its first decade, by the critical point in the industrial fortunes of the region when output in other parts of the country exceeded that of the Weald. It took only another 20 years before as much bar was made in the Weald as out of it, by which time sales of Wealden bar iron were dropping sharply and both furnaces and forges were being closed. By 1653 there were 35 furnaces working in the Weald, of which only 14 were active 11 years later, although another 12 were still in good repair. Of the forges over the same period, 19 went out of use permanently, out of 42, with only five idle but in working order. As much of the blame for this parlous state of affairs can be laid at the feet of James I's government as it can on the general growth of the iron industry throughout the rest of England and Wales.

The continued imposition of restrictions on the export of guns to the continent during the first two decades of the seventeenth century resulted in an embargo, for all practical purposes, taking effect in 1619. Until then, one of the principal markets for iron guns cast in the Weald – and there was only one furnace outside the Weald engaged in the same business – was the Netherlands. The Dutch, like the English, were a maritime nation, and ever since Queen Elizabeth's support for them in their struggle to overthrow their Spanish masters, they had been a ready market for guns to equip their overseas shipping fleet. The English ban on the export of iron ordnance hit the Dutch harder than most other countries. They had no heavy industry of their own; the industrial part of the Netherlands, in the southern part of what is now Belgium, still belonging to the Spanish. In the ensuing decades, Dutch entrepreneurs, led by Louis de Geer, sought to develop the iron industry that existed in Sweden, but which had continued to be operated on largely feudal lines. The combination of Dutch commercial organisation and the rich metallurgical resources available there resulted in the emergence of Sweden as a major manufacturer of iron cannon and, more crucially, of bar iron.

The embargo of 1619 substantially restricted the operations of the gunfounders. In 1615, John Browne had succeeded his father as royal gunfounder and, although his business was, to some extent, protected from the embargo because of his office, the casting of guns for export had been a useful way of keeping his furnaces busy. As the 1588 list had shown, furnaces were either engaged in casting sows for conversion into bar iron, or they were equipped for casting guns. It was not easy to switch between the two because of structural differences between the respective hearths for each operation so a gun-founding furnace needed to continue casting guns throughout a campaign. To this end, founders like John Browne would cast guns for merchant shipping or for export in between orders for the Crown. A reduction in orders would make sustaining a furnace in production difficult, and result in short, uneconomic campaigns. Another problem was the limited demand for iron guns by the Crown. Despite Wealden iron ordnance having a good reputation and being highly sought after by foreign states, the government, and the navy in particular, were slow to adopt them for general use. When the *Sovereign of the Seas* was built in 1638, the largest ship of its time, it was armed with bronze guns. Even during Henry VIII's reign, iron cannon purchased by the Crown had been deployed on shore fortifications, and when Elizabeth I's fleet sailed against the Armada, it was only the privateers which had been requisitioned to augment the fleet that carried cast-iron guns, while her navy was armed with wrought iron and bronze pieces.

To make matters worse for Browne, in February 1621 a patent was granted to Sir Sackville Crowe, a courtier, giving him the sole right to make iron guns for the merchant shipping of the kingdom. Only two years earlier he had been suspected of trying to export guns and a warrant had been issued for his arrest. His other connection with gunfounding seems to have been that he had succeeded his father in the occupation of the furnace at Maresfield, in Sussex. Browne's position became even less tenable. The one market still available to him which would have enabled him to sustain his furnaces alongside the limited orders placed by the Crown or when the occasional export licences was granted, had been taken from him. Wealden gunfounding had been reduced to the output of a pair of furnaces. Crowe achieved his position through the patronage of the Duke of Buckingham, a favourite of the King, but even though Buckingham died in 1628, the duopoly continued in force for another four years. Browne stood to lose the most. Gunfounding was a high-risk business. It involved heavy capital commitment and difficult cash flow management because of the slow settlement of accounts by the government. High standards were expected and there was a high failure rate, which could usually be offset by founders selling sub-standard guns to merchant vessels. However, with the monopoly of the civilian trade in the hands of Sir Sackville Crowe, the King's gunfounder, John Browne had no easy outlet for guns that were unsuitable for royal service.

Resigned to the navy's reluctance to abandon the use of cast bronze weapons, John Browne tried to find an opening into the potentially lucrative market of naval weaponry in the 1620s. Bronze had a weight advantage over iron and, in the small vessels of the period, it made good sense to retain the use of bronze if it could be afforded. However, merchants, who used smaller sizes of guns on their ships anyway, were attracted by the cheaper price of iron guns. John Browne began to experiment with casting lighter iron guns. By reducing the thickness of the metal, by shortening the barrel length or by altering the shape of the bore (the so-called 'drakes'), he sought to match the bronze guns that the navy favoured, weight for weight. He met with some success and, in 1626, the year after King Charles's accession, he was rewarded with £200 for achieving the production of a batch of iron guns which were lighter than their bronze counterparts. Browne also experimented with the type of metal he used, and references to 'fine metal' appear in the state papers at the end of the 1620s. The success of some of these experiments, notably of the 'drakes', made the guns attractive to merchants and the government was disquieted by the prospect of these revolutionary, if somewhat inaccurate, weapons falling into the wrong hands.

A major programme of shipbuilding, initiated by the Crown in 1632, offered some hope for the gunfounding industry, but this optimism was short-lived when it became clear that the new vessels would be armed almost entirely with bronze guns. John Browne's response was to offer to cast bronze guns at his works in Brenchley. The offer was accepted and by mid 1634 casting was underway. Perhaps the alacrity with which his offer had been taken up was a reflection of the dearth of bronze founders then available. Not only was his offer to cast in bronze taken up, but he was also granted a monopoly in the casting of iron guns. While Browne did some important work in bronze, most notably the armament for the *Sovereign of the Seas* in 1638, for which he supplied £23,525 worth of guns, his main business continued to be in iron.

The worsening political situation in England at the beginning of the 1640s, and the outbreak of hostilities between Parliament and the King, probably had little effect on the iron industry in the Weald as a whole, for it was through merchants that most of the iron was sold, and it was the political affiliation of the merchants that determined which side the iron reached. As royal gunfounder, however, John Browne's situation was more difficult. Undoubtedly he supplied the Royalist side during the early stages of the Civil War, and his employees were released from impressment for the King's service so that they could fulfil orders for guns. As the area under the control of the King moved west and away from London, Browne was granted the use of the royal ironworks in the Forest of Dean, but problems with access caused by the former tenant, and possibly a reluctance to ally himself too closely with the Royalist cause, made him decline the offer and re-assign the lease. The Parliamentarian side accused John Browne of allowing some of his workers to go to Oxford to assist in the casting of guns there, and Browne and his son, John, were closely examined on the matter of their loyalty in 1645. However, Browne was too valuable for Parliament not to make use of him, and in December of the same year the House of Commons decided that he should be allowed to retain control of his business. In collaboration with his son-in-law, Thomas Foley, an ironmaster from the West Midlands, John Browne

41 St Leonard's forge house, near Horsham

consolidated his position. The demand for orders enabled him to take short leases of other furnaces, including those at Cowden and Barden.

The conflict between the Crown and Parliament affected the ironworks in the Weald where ownership lay with the Crown. Parliament's dominance of south-east England meant that efforts were made to put out of use any works where it was thought the Crown was likely to draw supplies, or where the owners or ironmasters had Royalist sympathies. The royal works in St Leonard's Forest, near Horsham, were leased to Sir John Caryll, but were reported to have been damaged, as was the forge at Ifield, by a detachment of Parliamentary troops in late 1643, following the siege of Arundel (*41*). The forges in St Leonard's Forest were subsequently repaired and were in good order when surveyed in 1655. The works at Ifield seem not have been used again, being rebuilt as a corn mill about 20 years later.

John Browne maintained his monopoly after the end of the Civil War and it is somewhat ironic that, after all the problems of the previous three decades, when he had struggled to get iron guns accepted by the navy, he should die just as the navy's first true test of iron ordnance should begin. John Browne died in 1651 and his business was continued by his son, George, initially with Thomas Foley. For a short while they diversified their operations to include products such as domestic ironware as well as guns. However, by the following year, the worsening situation with the Dutch caused the Commonwealth government to order a large increase in naval strength – ironically a factor which had divided King and Parliament 10 years earlier. With that increase came orders for guns. Browne and Foley already had several guns cast and ready, but such was the demand that orders were placed with other founders, such as Nathaniel Powell, who owned Brede furnace. Orders came thick and fast, with Browne and Foley supplying home-bored guns and drakes in both fine and coarse metal. The heavy iron guns of the English fleet proved crucial in defeating the Dutch. With typical abruptness, the Treaty of Westminster, of 1654, which brought the conflict to a halt, also caused orders to cease. In May that year, a general reckoning was made of the guns that had been cast. In two years, Browne and Foley had received orders for 900 guns, of which 390 had been received, 430 were yet to be proved and only 80 had not been cast. Powell had been contracted for 650 pieces, though only a quarter of them had been received. The stimulus to the gun trade had been enormous, and the effectiveness of the cast-iron gun as a naval weapon established beyond doubt.

Ten years later, with King Charles II restored to the throne, Britain was again at war with the Dutch, and again George Browne and his brother John were the principal gunfounders; this time joined by Alexander Courthope. To cope with the demands, and to supplement the output from his own at Brenchley, Browne leased several other furnaces: Barden, Hawkhurst and Bedgebury in Kent, Ashburnham in Sussex, and Imbhams in Surrey. The last of these was some distance from the others, near Haslemere, and early in the Civil War the Quennells had been engaged in casting guns and shot there for the Royalist cause, but had been stopped. It was under the later occupancy of the Yalden family, who supported Parliament, that the Brownes were able to lease it. Each furnace was used to cast the size of guns it was most suited to. For example, Ashburnham was capable of casting guns of all sizes, while Hawkhurst was smaller and could cast nothing larger than 12-pounders. Some of these furnaces had appeared on a list of ironworks in the Weald made in 1653, where they had been recorded as no longer in use, so the demand for guns had resulted in their revival. The urgency of the situation caused somewhat of a panic at the Office of Ordnance.

> The Dutch are preparing speedily to come out to encounter his Majesty's fleet and there being severall ships now ready to go forth and doe stay for demi-cannon and culverins. His Majesty hath commanded that we doe forthwith send away all that are cast & bored of those natures …

So wrote George Browne to his brother John in February 1665. Yet they rose to the occasion, casting over 2500 tons of guns for the Office of Ordnance in that year, including bronze pieces, which they continued to produce at Brenchley.

Many of the same furnaces were put to use again when war against the Dutch broke out for a third time in the 1670s. Hamsell furnace, near

Rotherfield, was brought into the group as well. However, the Brownes' monopoly of gunfounding was diminishing. The Farnden family had made a range of iron products at Conster furnace, Beckley, before the Civil War, but they too had begun to make guns there and at their other furnace, at Crowhurst, during the Dutch wars.

It is in this period that a curious sideline to the gunfounding industry occurred. In the 1620s and 30s, John Browne had explored a number of ways to improve the metal from which guns were cast, and in the 1650s both he and Nathaniel Powell were producing guns from 'fine' and 'coarse' metal. Precisely how these guns differed is not clear. In 1671, Prince Rupert of the Rhine, former dashing cavalry commander during the Civil War, was granted a patent for a method of transforming cast iron so that it could be treated like wrought iron. As has already been noted, cast iron is chemically different from wrought iron, making it brittle and unstable in tension, although strong in compression (when it is used in castings such as cannon). However, it is very hard, and difficult to drill out or file. Cast bronze, on the other hand, is more easily worked and capable of being 'finished' to a high degree of precision. Experiments carried out for the Prince, under the auspices of the Office of Ordnance, went on during the next two years, by which time John Browne, nephew of George Browne, and Thomas Western, another gunfounder, had become involved, although in the case of the latter, only temporarily. By the end of 1673, the Office of Ordnance placed an order with John Browne for 'New Turn'd Iron Ordnance', at a price of £60 per ton. Normal iron guns cost between £16 and £22 a ton at the time.

For the next three years, only these special turned guns seem to have been ordered by the Office, and although they were originally ordered for specific ships, the Brownes continued casting them for general stock. However, in 1677 the Office of Ordnance, presumably recognising belatedly that they were paying far too high a price, stopped issuing warrants for the 'Neal'd and Turned' guns as they had come to be called and reverted to guns of ordinary cast iron. This had serious consequences for the Brownes. They had continued casting these expensive guns in anticipation of their eventual purchase by the government and had consequently over-reached themselves financially to the tune of over £11,000. John Browne had died in 1677 and it was left to his widow, Mary, Alexander Courthope's daughter, to settle with the creditors. Eventually such a settlement was reached but not before the Browne family, who had been involved in the gun trade for nearly a century, had retired from the business.

The second half of the seventeenth century saw a marked reduction in the number of forges in the Weald, and with them of the number of furnaces. As a consequence of the 1619 embargo on the export of guns and the efforts by Dutch entrepreneurs to revitalise and develop the Swedish iron industry, by 1640 the Swedes were exporting around 11,000 tons of iron a year. Between

1650 and 1670 an average of 4000 tons of Swedish iron was being imported into England annually. The biggest areas of growth in the iron industry were in the west and north of England and in South Wales. The high cost of overland transport meant that the largest market for iron – London, which had been a major outlet for Wealden bar iron – was not within easy reach of many of the new iron-producing districts, like the Severn valley, South Wales and Yorkshire. However, the Swedish iron imports came by sea, a much more economic mode of transport and, with prices that were highly competitive, London became a major importer of Swedish iron at the Weald's expense.

The contraction in the bar iron trade affected the nature of industry in the region. As the iron produced in the Weald became less important nationally, the traditional relationships between works began to change. Furnaces and forges less well supplied with wood and ore closed down. A few were seen as attractive investments by outsiders, such as London ironmongers, and a greater realism began to affect the conduct of the trade in the region. A major set of accounts are those of the Pelhams, who owned Bivelham forge, east of Mayfield, and Glazier's forge near Brightling. Although they also had a furnace at Waldron, the distances between their works were such that it was more efficient to operate each works with some degree of independence rather than attempt to supply the forges solely from the furnace. So Waldron furnace sold some of its pig iron to forges within easier reach, and the Pelham forges drew some of their sows from furnaces that were more conveniently located for them than Waldron. Wealden forges were capable of making over 100 tons of wrought iron a year, but the lists that were drawn up at the beginning of the eighteenth century indicate that few were achieving more than half that amount.

However, the iron founders of the region had built up a reputation for the production of guns, and in this business they had further advantages. The main market was London, with the naval dockyards at Chatham and Portsmouth also near at hand. The skilled labour force and the legacy of those skills were firmly based in the Weald, and furnaces were already adapted to the task. Therefore, while the regular business of iron-making – the production of sows and their refining into bars – diminished in importance, gunfounding took on a greater significance. The wars against the Dutch demonstrated the superiority of English iron guns, to the extent that, from then on, no British naval vessel was armed ever again with bronze weaponry. However, the seventeenth century was the time when Britain began to colonise the parts of the world that had been discovered in the preceding 100 years. Many of the great trading companies, such as the Merchant Adventurers and the Africa and Muscovy Companies, were established in the late Tudor period. Perhaps the greatest of them all, the East India Company, founded in 1600, had, since its inception, purchased guns made in the Weald for its forts and factories in the Far East. During the early part of the seventeenth century, colonists had begun to open up the eastern seaboard of America.

Carolina, Pennsylvania and the puritan colonies of New England all came in to being during this period. Whether it was to defend their newly won territories or to protect the ships that carried the supplies and personnel to and from them, the common requirement was iron guns. This increasing demand enabled many furnaces in the Weald to continue to be active, but the nature of the demand was also reflected in a change in the people who began to operate the furnaces. From the mid sixteenth century, the ironmasters in the Weald had been essentially local in origin. The Brownes, for instance, started their involvement in the gun trade at Chiddingstone, in Kent, before settling at Horsmonden. The concentration on the merchant trade in guns brought the merchants themselves into the business.

One of the first of these was Thomas Western. Born in 1624, he was established as an ironmonger by 1650 when he married Martha, the youngest daughter of Samuel Gott, a fellow London ironmonger. The Gotts already had connections with the iron industry in the Weald through Martha's brother, Samuel, who had married Joan, one of the 12 daughters of Peter Farnden, the ironmaster at Beckley. In 1660, Thomas Western took a lease of the furnace at Brede, and in 1664 when increasing tension in relations with the Dutch was making war inevitable, the government placed an order with him for round shot and guns. The Brownes had been unable to meet the demands placed upon them, which led to Western and another Wealden ironmaster, John Newnham who had Maresfield furnace, being issued with warrants. In addition to contracts for the Office of Ordnance, Western also began to cast guns for the East India Company. In the 1670s Western took a lease of Ashburnham furnace so that he could cope with additional orders from the government for the new 'Neal'd and Turned' guns that had been developed, and which the Brownes may not have been able to fulfil.

Western continued to cast guns for the government through the reigns of James II and William and Mary. By the 1690s, though, Thomas Western was becoming an old man and was already beginning to hand over control of his business to his sons. With war again being waged against the French, government demand for guns increased. Other gunfounders were beginning to enter the trade, such as William Benge, of Wadhurst, and Western's son-in-law, Peter Gott, who were working in partnership. The 1690s saw the Wealden gunfounding trade in buoyant condition. Demand was high and, like the Brownes three decades earlier, William Benge expanded his business by taking short leases of other works to enable him to complete his warrants for the Office of Ordnance. The Gott family had acquired the Hoathly forge at Lamberhurst, and in 1695, with their support, Benge petitioned the government to assist him in financing the building of a new furnace there. The prestigious new structure was reckoned the largest in the region. Later visited by the Duke of Gloucester, son of the future Queen Anne, it came to be known as the Gloucester Furnace. Peter Gott also operated ironworks in his own right, having acquired by inheritance the works once owned by his grandfather, Peter Farnden.

The furnace at Lamberhurst was not the only one to be built in the Weald at the time. Two years earlier, John Fuller, a major in the Trained Bands, or militia, had acquired land at Heathfield and built a new furnace. Fuller's family had been involved in the iron industry since 1650 when his grandfather had leased Stream furnace, at Chiddingly, where he had cast guns during the crisis of the Second Dutch War. The third new furnace, at Pippingford, in Hartfield, which dates from 1696, was built on land newly enclosed from Ashdown Forest. The entrepreneurs involved, James Hooper and Francis Diggs, were London merchants, but they do not seem to have operated the furnace themselves, leasing it out to Charles Manning. In fact two furnaces were built there. The first was equipped for gun casting, but its replacement was not, perhaps reflecting the changing economic circumstances of the time. The demand for guns at the end of the seventeenth century did not last for long. With peace came a slump in the ordnance trade and ironworks returned to the business of casting sows for bar iron production at their forges. Some furnaces, including the new ones at Pippingford, inevitably went out of business. Just such a state of affairs confronted John Fuller and Samuel Gott. While they were adjusting to the change in market at their new furnaces at Heathfield and Lamberhurst, Maximilian Western had not renewed the lease of Ashburnham furnace that his father had held. Lord Ashburnham was keen to find a new tenant and, in 1706, his son, William, approached two ironmasters from outside the Weald. Ambrose Crowley was becoming a major figure in the iron industry nationally. Developing his father's Midlands-based ironmongery business, he had built mills on Tyneside for the production of wrought iron wares, using Swedish iron, and had become a significant supplier of ironwork to the navy. John Hanbury, of Pontypool, operated ironworks in South Wales, producing bar and rod iron, the latter for the nail trade, as well as iron plate. Although Crowley offered to purchase iron made at the furnace, neither of them was willing to have a lease. Two years were to elapse before a suitable tenant could be found, and again it was from outside the Weald. Thomas Foley had, through marriage, become a partner of John Browne in the mid seventeenth century, but his family had built up an extensive iron-making business in the Forest of Dean and Severn valley. By the 1690s a partnership to operate this business had been formed which included members of the Foley family and others. Among them was William Rea of Monmouth. It was Rea, on behalf of the Forest Partnership, as they were called, who purchased a seven-year lease of Ashburnham furnace, and Westfield forge which belonged to Peter Gott. Acting for Rea in the negotiations was Thomas Hussey, at the beginning of a career in the Weald which was to continue for the next 27 years.

Hussey was born in Worcestershire, where his father had been an ironmaster. It is not known why or when he moved to Sussex, but he became clerk at Ashburnham and Westfield for the Forest Partnership, accounting to them over the next few years for iron pigs and sows, and other cast and wrought iron products. These were sold to local forges as well as those further afield, among others, to Sir Ambrose Crowley, London ironmongers and the partnership's forges via Bewdley, on the River Severn. A two-year embargo on the import of Swedish iron, starting in 1717, boosted trade briefly, but the Forest Partnership may have already withdrawn from Ashburnham and Westfield by then. The following year, Hussey took on the Pelham family ironworks at Bivelham forge, Mayfield, at Glazier's forge, Brightling, and at Waldron furnace. In the next decade he was joined by John Legas, who had come from the same neighbourhood as Hussey on the Shropshire border and who had been managing the furnace at Lamberhurst for Samuel Gott. They took leases there and at Chingley forge. They extended their operations by becoming partners with the Gotts at Beckley furnace and Westfield forge. When Thomas Hussey died at Burwash in 1735 he was involved, either directly or through partnerships, in nine furnaces and forges.

Another important figure in the Wealden iron industry in the eighteenth century was William Harrison, who had been one of the purchasers of iron from Ashburnham. His involvement in the region dated back to 1708 when guns cast by Robert Baker at Hamsell furnace, Rotherfield, had come into his hands at the wharf he had by the River Thames at Southwark. Harrison was a Derbyshire-born merchant and ironmonger who had also worked for the Board of Ordnance, which purchased weapons and stores for the navy and army. In 1721, he diversified his business by taking over Brede furnace from Maximilian Western. Shortly after this occurred the death of Samuel Gott. Gott had taken an active role in the iron industry, owning the Gloucester furnace at Lamberhurst, Conster furnace at Beckley and Westfield forge. He was succeeded by his brother Maximilian. The use by the Westerns and Gotts of this Christian name betrays their close family ties; Maximilian Gott's grandfather was Thomas Western, Gott's mother being Maximilian Western's sister. Gott was less involved in the industry than his brother had been, so a partnership was formed by which Gott's works could be brought into a more integrated group of furnaces and forges operated by Thomas Hussey, John Legas, William Harrison and another newcomer, William Jukes, who was also a London ironmonger.

The change in the personnel who were controlling the operation of furnaces in the Weald, from locally based to London based, had been under way since the 1670s, but there were still a small number of ironmasters whose centres of operation remained in the region. The Ashburnhams had been involved, on and off, since the 1550s, with their works forming part of their landed estate. More recent in their acquisition of land were the Fullers, who had lived in Waldron, and who had joined the iron trade in partnership with Sir Thomas Dyke. John Fuller (1680-1745) married an heiress and came into a fortune which included sugar plantations in Jamaica. He moved to Brightling and the furnace his father had built at Heathfield in 1693 produced pig iron and guns, according to demand, throughout the first 40 years of the century. The guns were sold to the government and the pig iron sent to the Fullers' forge at Burwash or sold to a number of other forges that were operating independently in Sussex at that time. These included Tinsley, Maresfield and Etchingham. Other castings were also made at Heathfield, some of which, like hammers and anvils, were directly related to the iron trade, while others, such as garden rollers and pots, were for the domestic market. Sugar rollers were cast, probably for the Fullers' own estates in the West Indies. During this same period, John Butler, who was also from a local family, although not the owner of a large estate, seems to have become active in the western end of the Weald. Most of the furnaces in that part had closed down during the seventeenth century, but a couple – Burningfold, near Dunsfold, and North Park, near Fernhurst, along with their associated forges – had remained in operation. Butler may have occupied both, but is more definitely associated with the latter. It is not clear why, in 1738, he attempted to purchase some guns from John Fuller. Whether he had started to cast guns himself and needed to complete an order, or was merely dealing and needed a supplier, is not known. The last of the ironmasters active in the years leading up to the outbreak of war in 1739 was William Bowen. Nothing is known, at present, of how he came to be in the iron business, but he was operating a forge and furnace at Barden, near Tonbridge, from about 1729 and was buying iron from the Fullers. Like William Harrison and William Jukes, he also had a yard beside the Thames.

In 1734, William Harrison took a joint lease of Robertsbridge furnace with William Jukes and his brother, George. They leased the forge three years later. The Jukes brothers had probably been working the furnace for a few years before then and there is evidence that they too, had been operating Burningfold furnace some time previously. A few years later, Theodosia Crowley, whose father-in-law had declined to operate the furnace at Ashburnham 30 years earlier, took a lease for the site and for Darwell furnace at Mountfield. It would seem that their intention was to produce pig iron for forging at their Tyneside works. At a relatively peaceful time, indeed one of the longest periods of peace for a century, it is remarkable that the Weald was continuing to attract such investment, despite the leases generally being for short periods. But all that was to change.

In 1739 the so-called War of Jenkins' Ear presaged a longer conflict waged on the disputed succession to the throne of Austria. Tensions had been rising, particularly where there was competition for colonial supremacy, such as in India and North America. Demand for guns for the navy increased and orders were placed with founders whose furnaces were suitably equipped and manned. John Fuller, who had been a regular supplier throughout

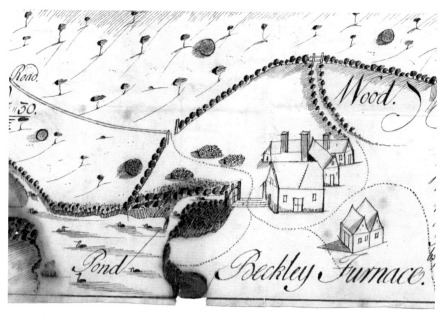

42 Beckley furnace in 1746, detail (*East Sussex Record Office, Lewes, ACC 165-1526*)

the preceding years, William Harrison and William Jukes were all given contracts. However, one of the largest suppliers of ordnance during the war years to 1748 was Samuel Remnant. He was a key figure in the iron industry. He held the office of Master Smith to the Board of Ordnance and had his own works at Woolwich, near to the Royal Arsenal. However, he did not cast guns, but sub-contracted his orders to other founders who were almost certainly John Legas, who operated the furnace at Lamberhurst, and William Harrison. He and Legas had formed a partnership in 1741, which only ended when Harrison died four years later. Remnant also acted as agent at Woolwich for John Fuller and for William Bowen. In that role, he was able to report on the arrival of guns at the arsenal and on the outcome of their testing, or proof. He could also arrange sub-contracting with other ironmasters when guns were needed to make up orders. Another furnace that supplied guns during the war period was William Gott's at Beckley (*42*). Later in the 1740s, the Crowleys at Ashburnham began to cast guns, as did William Bowen, who had bought Cowden furnace in 1742.

The peace which came in 1748 was more a cessation of hostilities than a resolution of the causes of the conflict, and many of the issues, between the British and the French in particular, remained. So it is not altogether surprising that the younger John Fuller, who had succeeded his father as head of the family's iron-founding business in 1745, was able to continue supplying the government. He also supplied a few friendly foreign states, such as Naples, with ordnance throughout the following years. The prospect of renewed military and naval action, and the profitability of gunfounding during wartime encouraged iron founders to consider investment in the Weald. Such an individual was John Churchill, who had been based in the Midlands but who entered into negotiations to take a lease of the Robertsbridge ironworks when George Jukes decided not to renew in 1754. He also later took on Darwell furnace which the Crowleys no longer needed. When war did break out again two years later the effect on the Wealden iron industry was immediate. In the space of a year, the tonnage of guns cast increased fivefold, doubling again over the next three years as two other ironmasters established themselves. Edward Raby, a London ironmonger, refurbished the Warren furnace, near East Grinstead, which had lain idle for more than a century, and William Clutton, a local man with no known experience in the industry, set about constructing a new furnace at Gravetye, near West Hoathly. Clutton's gamble did not pay off and he was bankrupt within a year (43). The demand for guns increased to the point where ironmasters outside the Weald were being given contracts by the Board of Ordnance. This had happened in a few instances before, at the end of the seventeenth century and in the late 1740s when the furnace at Sowley, near Beaulieu in Hampshire, was favoured with contracts by its landlord, the Duke of Montagu, who was Master of the Ordnance. However, a problem which often beset such ventures was that of attracting sufficiently skilled founders and moulders. Due to a long tradition of gunfounding, the Weald was able to call upon a body of expertise which was not easily available elsewhere. Sometimes the workers that could be enticed from the Weald were less than suitable, as in the case of a founder named Betts, who went to work for Robert Morgan, who was casting guns at Carmarthen furnace in Wales. Through drunkenness, Betts caused the failure of a whole batch of guns, and Morgan had to get John Churchill, at Robertsbridge, to complete his order for him.

Gunfounders laboured under considerable difficulties, due to the exacting nature of their trade, which involved working under constant pressure to have a steady flow of moulds ready for casting, and at a time of the year which was least conducive to drying the moulds and to transporting the guns by road. The Board of Ordnance, their principal market, made life even harder by issuing its contracts, or warrants as they were called, at the beginning of the year, probably a third of the way through most furnace campaigns, when a programme of casting was probably already in place. Furthermore, the warrants were expected to be completed by the end of the year, during which there would be the usual hiatus in the summer when the furnaces would not be in blast because of the shortage of water, and any last-minute efforts to complete the warrants would be impeded by the winter rains again preventing guns being delivered on time. Finally, the Board was notoriously slow at paying; ironmasters had to wait for 15 months or more, during which time they were expected to pay their workforce and

43 Guns cast at Gravetye furnace, in the account book of a local carrier, 1762 (*West Sussex Record Office, Chichester, Add Ms 46861*)

the suppliers of their ore and charcoal. In these circumstances it is hardly surprising that Clutton's bankruptcy in 1762 was only the first. Edward Raby went under in 1764 and Churchill in 1768. The bankruptcy with the most far-reaching impact was that of Richard Tapsell. Harrison and Legas' partnership had continued, in a modified form, after Harrison's death, with the business carried on by Legas and Samuel Remnant, in trust for Harrison's two sons. Both Legas and Remnant died in 1752, and Legas' role was taken over by his niece's husband, Richard Tapsell, whom Legas had groomed as his successor. Harrison's sons, who were only in their early twenties, were being advised by Harrison's former manager, Robert Bagshaw. Since most of the ironworks controlled by the partnership had formerly been leased by John Legas, it was Tapsell who had become their nominal tenant. Legas' death had made him a rich man, but he lacked his mentor's business acumen and lost the fortune that had come his way. When he became bankrupt in 1765, at least seven furnaces or forges stopped work.

The Seven Years' War had seen the Wealden furnaces busier than they had been for nearly a century, and their importance as the main source of iron cannon in the kingdom confirmed. However, an event was to occur which would have a critical effect and, at a stroke, speed up the hitherto slow decline of the iron industry in the region. Within months of peace being declared in 1763, the Board of Ordnance received a tender for a large batch of cannon at nearly a third less than the price the Board had been paying hitherto. The Carron Company, of Falkirk in Scotland, had been established a few years earlier and had built several large furnaces, some powered by cylinders instead of bellows, and all fuelled with coke, the use of which was becoming increasingly widespread in the iron industry generally. The cost of charcoal had always formed the largest element in the expenditure of a Wealden ironworks, with the supply of ore being only a third as much. A majority of the cost of charcoal resulted from the labour involved. The work of digging for coke was comparable to that for ore. Although untried, the Carron offer was accepted, and Wealden ironmasters were asked to match it if they could. The first to react were the Fullers, who promptly withdrew from casting for the government after over a century of loyal service. The slump in demand for guns following the end of the war had meant that some furnaces had gone back to casting sows for forges. Some ironmasters, notably William Bowen, were able to match Carron's prices, but the degree to which Carron had undercut even the lower, peacetime prices expected by the operators of charcoal furnaces meant that it would be difficult to recover the position the Wealden gunfoundries had held only a year or two earlier. In fact, although Bowen continued to gain contracts, Carron dominated the government ordnance trade until the beginning of the 1770s.

Although contracts to supply guns for the Board of Ordnance were beyond the reach of most Wealden gunfounders, a number of furnaces in the region continued to produce guns for the merchant trade. Rose Fuller, who had returned from Jamaica to take over the family estate on the death of his brother in 1755, did not give up seeking ways in which his family's position as major gunfounders might be restored. So when, in the late 1760s, Carron guns began to fail the proof at Woolwich and, a few years later, started to burst at sea, leading to the Board of Ordnance ordering that all Carron guns should be removed from naval ships and replaced, it seemed that Fuller's chance had come. In the event, although the Carron Company had lost its contracts, the Board were only too aware that the price of coke-smelted iron cannon was significantly lower than those made using charcoal, so they sought out founders who would be able to hold to the lower price. A few warrants were issued to Wealden ironmasters in this period: Joseph Wright and Thomas Prickett had leased the North Park furnace, near Fernhurst, before taking over furnaces formerly occupied by Edward Raby and Richard Tapsell, and James Bourne had continued working Robertsbridge furnace in place of his kinsmen, John Churchill and son. At Ashburnham, where her daughter, Elizabeth, had married the Earl of Ashburnham, Theodosia Crowley's company continued to cast guns. This situation, more or less, came to an end in 1775 when the Board of Ordnance became convinced that cannon cast solid and then bored out, using a new boring machine patented by the Shropshire ironmaster John Wilkinson, were better than ones cast hollow, as had been the Wealden practice since the 1540s. Although boring mills were to be found wherever there were gun-founding furnaces in the Weald, the modest water supply that most of the region's furnaces relied upon was not sufficient to generate the greater horsepower needed for the new boring machines. Despite this setback, the Fullers in particular persisted in trying to get the Board to accept their guns, eventually succeeding in 1779 when they supplied 62 four-pounders and half-pounders. Crowley & Co., at Ashburnham, continued to cast guns for merchant ships, notably for the East India Company, which could still be made in the traditional way, the last ones being proved in 1789.

Throughout the middle years of the eighteenth century, when the Weald's furnaces had been almost solely engaged in casting guns, a more or less equal number of forges had continued to operate. Some of these were directly linked to furnaces, such as Burwash forge and Heathfield furnace, Woodcock Hammer and Warren furnace, and Pophole Hammer and North Park furnace. In the case of Robertsbridge, the forge and furnace were only a short distance apart, while Westfield and Glazier's forges were some distance from Brede and Beckley furnaces. At Ashburnham, the forge had been converted to a boring mill, the Crowleys' ironworks in north-east England being the destination for any sow iron made there, shipped out through Hastings. Although furnaces casting guns were not adapted for producing other types of casting, during the first few weeks of a campaign, after the furnace had been 'blown in', the iron was not considered to be of sufficient quality for casting into guns, so sows were cast instead, which were taken to the forge for converting into wrought iron. Even during gun casting, an extraneous piece of the metal, which was intended to collect any impurities and gas bubbles, was formed at the front of each gun in the mould. Known as the gunhead, it was sawn off and sent to the forge for fining. A third source of iron for forges were rejected castings where, through a faulty mould or misaligned nowel bar, a gun could not be sold on for use on a merchant ship but had to be broken up and used to make bar iron. Furnaces might also have to cast sows in-between batches of guns, if moulds were not ready, so that the unnecessary expense of the furnace being 'blown out' could be avoided. Thus, some forges could be kept in business, and a few of them operated independently of furnaces. Howbourne forge, at Buxted, Maresfield forge and Abinger Hammer were all operated by local ironmongers, who bought sow iron and gunheads from furnaces to make wrought iron for sale to local blacksmiths. Each was associated with a wholesale outlet: the first two in Lewes and the last in Guildford. When James Bourne took over Robertsbridge forge and furnace in 1768 it was in partnership with local ironmongers from Hastings and Rye.

The last few years of the Wealden iron industry saw a small number of furnaces and forges with fewer and fewer markets. North Park furnace, the last to operate in the western Weald, and its forge at Pophole, near Haslemere, closed in 1776 following the bankruptcy of James Goodyer. Heathfield, as has already been noted, cast its last guns in 1779, and continued producing iron

44 Cast-iron lintel from Lamberhurst furnace, 1696

sows for any forges that would buy them, and some domestic ironware, until 1787 when it was blown out for the last time. Its forge at Burwash kept going on scrap and pig iron until 1803. The Gloucester furnace at Lamberhurst, the largest furnace of its time, was revived briefly by William Collins in 1783 to cast a quantity guns, but the project was abandoned after only five months when it was found to be no longer viable. When it was demolished in about 1795, the iron lintel that supported the casting arch, and which bore the date 1696, and the initials of William Benge and his wife, Dinah, was removed to Hoathly Farm nearby and survives to this day above the kitchen range (*44*). Robertsbridge does not seem to have worked after 1801, leaving Ashburnham alone to carry on. Its forge was converted back to its proper use in 1789 and the furnace closed in early 1813, a batch of firebacks being its last products. The occasion was marred, however, by the tragic death of a six-year-old boy from alcohol poisoning as the ironworkers drank to the end of an era. Ashburnham forge, the last ironworks in the Weald, continued in sporadic use for another 14 years, surviving on scrap iron or imported pig, and closed in 1827.

6

ECONOMIC EFFECTS OF
IRON-MAKING

THE WORKFORCE

The backbone of the iron industry was its workforce which, throughout the long period during which iron was being made in the Weald, performed manual labour, often of a very arduous form. Whether it was digging ore, cutting and carrying wood or manoeuvring cast or wrought iron, the weights involved could be very demanding, and the mechanical aids relatively minimal. Animal power was utilised where possible, but the landscape itself, its steep slopes and soils that were often unforgiving when wet, made much of the work all the harder. The majority of the workforce, in all the periods, was unskilled and the principal tasks remained the same whether during the Roman occupation or the wars of the mid eighteenth century. The source of the unskilled labour will have varied from one period to another, as will the number.

Digging, or drawing, ore largely involved removing a large quantity of overburden, containing sandstone, limestone or clay, and a relatively small percentage of ore. As has been noted in Chapter 1, the method of ore extraction varied between the Roman period and the medieval and post-medieval. The apparent Roman practice of ore extraction from quarries probably involved a greater labour force and was more efficient. Later, the rights of individual landowners dictated that a different approach was adopted. Ore digging took place in the summer to avoid the pits filling with water, and pits would be dug starting at the lowest level in the landscape first, again to minimise the collection of water flowing in from pits further uphill. Probably three men would dig a pit, taking it in turns to dig, shovel and raise the containers of ore or clay to the surface. The diameter of the pits makes it unlikely that there would have been room for more people digging in each pit. Once the ore had been dug out, the pit was refilled, probably with the contents of the next pit to be dug close by. In a section of a 12m minepit sunk in the Wadhurst Clay at Sharpthorne, the cumulative depth of the layers of ore amounted to about

0.5m, so digging would have necessitated removing in the order of 145m³ of clay to recover just over 6m³ of ore – a lot of work for a very modest return. On that basis, one pit might provide enough ore to make two tons of iron, so digging two pits every three days would just about keep a blast furnace supplied, and about 150 pits would need to be dug for a single campaign at a large furnace such as the one at Heathfield.

Being what is known to historians as a wood-pasture area, the Weald supported agriculture that was geared to fattening cattle and wood-related occupations. The amount of arable farming was limited because of poor soils, and the generally weak influence of landed estates, compared to areas like the Downs, attracted a population that was independent and inclined of necessity to undertake a variety of occupations depending on the time of year. Those engaged in digging for ore would have also been farm labourers, turning their hands to woodland crafts, like hurdle- and besom-making and other labouring jobs at ironworks. The accounts of furnaces and forges from the Middle Ages onwards include references to many jobs, such as repairing woodwork or brickwork, digging sand or loam for casting, and clearing out water channels. Some of the basic labouring jobs were paid out of the wages of the principal skilled workers, like the founder, so many of the tasks go unrecorded.

Charcoal-making was carried out by colliers; workers operating in an area who were engaged by the ironmaster to cut and coal the woods that had been leased for the purpose. In the first half of the eighteenth century, the clerk at Robertsbridge furnace wrote, in a memorandum on the making of iron, that he urged his successor to ensure that the woodcutters completed their work by the end of January, well before the new growth began. The colliers who would make the charcoal should not, he wrote, have all the wood made available to them at once, to discourage them from selling the charcoal elsewhere. Colliers sought employment throughout the year, but ironmasters wanted their services during the autumn and winter only so that the charcoal was of good quality, and to build up resources for the campaign that would start in the following autumn. The ironmaster's and the collier's interests were not always mutually compatible.

One other group of workers, whose iron-related tasks were carried out alongside agricultural employment, were those involved in the transport of raw materials and products. Wagons or sledges hauled by teams of oxen or horses occupied a large number of people. The weight of iron sows or cannon meant that only small numbers could be carried at a time, so frequent journeys, sometimes over long distances, were necessary.

We know nothing about the ownership or operation of ironworks in the pre-Roman Iron Age, and not much more from during the Roman occupation. Rights to all mineral extraction belonged to the emperor, so some system must have existed whereby iron-makers either paid some sort of licence to a local level of administration or contributed a portion of their production. An inscription referring to a *collegium fabrorum*, or guild of smiths, which was found at Chichester, suggests some organisation in that city, but the distance between there and the nearest ironworking area in the Weald makes a connection between them unlikely. We are on slightly safer ground with the organisation of the *Classis Britannica*, the British Fleet, who were operating some of the large ironworks in the south-eastern Weald. The fleet was akin to a legion, with units formed of crews, rather than the centuries of the legions. At the head of the fleet was the Prefect, a title held, in its early days, by the Procurator of the province of Britain. At a local level, the only evidence for any individuals associated with the fleet comes from the partial inscription found at Beauport Park ironworks which may relate to the enlargement of the bath house by Bassus or Bassanus, under orders from the *vilicus*, or manager (45).

The management of ironworks in the medieval and post-medieval periods did not differ from each other in any significant way. The landowner, whether one of the great estates of the realm or someone humbler, could either operate the ironworks 'in hand', employing a skilled manager, or could lease the works to someone else, usually an ironmaster. Lady Elizabeth de Burgh's estate stewards managed the works at Tudeley in the fourteenth century; a job which they were probably glad to hand over to Thomas Springet, who was clearly more experienced as he had leased the works himself previously. Managing an ironworks was not dissimilar to managing any other

45 Beauport Park bath house inscription; Battle Museum

undertaking, but it helped to have background knowledge of the industry. William Levett, a clergyman and Receiver of the King's Revenues, was clearly an educated man, but he had the advantage that his brother had operated ironworks, and presumably he had gained the necessary understanding of the iron industry from him. Incidentally, the term, ironmaster has been used frequently in these pages. Its earliest historical use is probably in a deed of 1606 where William Relfe, of Penhurst, who leased Ashburnham furnace and forge, was so described. It refers to the person who has full managerial control of an ironworks, making the profit and bearing the loss, employing the workers and having responsibility for sourcing the raw materials and marketing the products. Landowners often leased their ironworks to ironmasters who, themselves, may have been landowners through the wealth that the iron industry could generate. Even in the 1550s, when Robertsbridge and Panningridge were operated 'in hand' by Sir William Sidney, the profit for the year was over £1200; equivalent to a quarter of a million pounds in modern money. The other side of the huge profits that could be made from iron-making was the loss that a bad investment or bad management could lead to. The real possibility of debt existed, as in the case of Peter Roberts at Newbridge in the late fifteenth century, who ended up in prison. Bankruptcy was also a possibility and afflicted several ironmasters in the eighteenth century.

The skilled workers at the ironworks at Tudeley were the blowers, or foreblowers; amusingly, there were four of them. Their role would have been to control the smelting process, not merely blowing the air into the furnace but also regulating the amount of ore and charcoal, and judging when the process was complete and when the bloom could be withdrawn. The *factor ferri* recorded in Crawley in the 1370s may have been more akin to the later title of ironmaster.

At the blast furnace, the principal skilled worker was the founder, who was in charge of preparing and tapping the hearth, casting the iron, and would have controlled the flow of water to power the bellows. He was paid well and would have paid some of the unskilled workmen under him from his fee. As the furnace was operated 24 hours a day, seven days a week for several months of the year, and sometimes longer, the founder would have had a deputy, or under-founder, so that at least one of them would have been on duty at any one time when the furnace was in blast. The same was necessary of the filler, whose job was to prepare the ore and charcoal and charge the furnace when required; there would be an under-filler. Where guns were being cast, a key job was that of moulder who, as the name implies, supervised the making of cannon moulds. The need to prepare moulds ready for casting each time the hearth of the furnace was full meant that a sort of production line was necessary. A moulder would need several assistants so that there would always be moulds at different stages of preparation. The greater manpower needed for gunfounding is reflected in John Browne's claim that he had 200 workers ready at his furnace at Horsmonden in the seventeenth century, although he may have been exaggerating for effect. John Fuller, when seeking government ordnance contracts, referred to 50 workers at his furnace standing idle for want of work. Extra accommodation was needed to house such a workforce.

The principal workers at the finery forge were the finer and the hammerman. The finers, for there were sometimes two of these, were, as their title suggests, in charge of remelting the sows brought from the furnace and producing a bloom of wrought iron. This the hammerman, working at the chafery hearth, would form into an iron bar. As at the furnace, the various labouring tasks of moving materials and assisting the finer or hammerman would be carried out by additional workmen. No deputies were needed at the forge as work could be suspended overnight. Specialist ironworkers are occasionally noted in the archives. Steel-makers were recorded at Robertsbridge and in Hartfield. Potfounders, skilled in casting using closed moulds, also occur. Other specialists included repairers of bellows. With the blast furnace and forge being introduced from France, many of the skilled ironworkers initially were French and, as time went on, and skills were often passed down through families, many such workers remained of foreign extraction. Although there were instances of formal apprenticeships, such as that of William Roberts, who was apprenticed to John Bartholomew, the hammerman at Tinsley forge in 1616, much of the training for the skilled ironworkers was informal and probably family based. That is not to say that all skilled ironworkers were of French origin. It has been suggested that Langley's furnace, one the works operated by Ralph Hogge, derived its name from *l'Anglais*, 'the English furnace', differentiating it from those worked by Frenchmen.

Estimates of the total workforce engaged in the iron industry in the Weald are difficult because only a small number of workers are accounted for in payments made for specific jobs. At Ashburnham, in the campaign which ended in 1759, about 60 individuals were named in the accounts as having been paid for a variety of work. If it is assumed that others would have been paid by them, perhaps half as many people again should added to that number, bringing the total to nearer 90, which falls between John Browne's and John Fuller's claims. Their furnaces, as well as Ashburnham, were casting guns, so the team of moulders augmented the number of their workers beyond that of a furnace casting sows. For a furnace casting for the forge, a workforce nearer 75 might be reasonable. In addition, the forge had its own workers, but these would have been considerably fewer; perhaps a quarter of the number. In 1574 there were 50 furnaces and 50 forges, of which only about eight were casting guns, giving a total workforce at the time of close to 6000, compared with a possible Wealden population of about 70,000.

BUILDINGS

Two main types of building were associated with the iron industry: working and residential. The former included the furnace stack, with its associated casting and blowing houses, and possibly a bridge house, which covered the charging bridge from the valley side or pond bay to the top of the furnace. Furnaces have already been described. Earlier ones had a wooden framework around them which would have been made flat on the ground and then hoisted into position, much as the sides of a timber house would have been. At Chingley furnace, the corners of the stack were rebated to hold the frame. The casting and blowing houses would have been simple timber-framed barns with their bays adjusted to fit round the stack. Continental illustrations of early blast furnaces show these buildings as being thatched, which seems rather hazardous given the close proximity of the top of the furnace (46). What evidence there is of the roofs of such buildings in the Weald suggests that tiles were used instead. Gun-casting furnaces would have had a boring mill; in some cases close to the furnace, such as at Warren furnace and at Lamberhurst and Mayfield. Sometimes these were located at the associated forge. As gun boring was a slow business, it was not uncommon for furnaces casting large numbers of guns to have two boring mills: Ashburnham, Heathfield and Robertsbridge are examples. At Robertsbridge, in the eighteenth century, the boring mills were housed in two buildings, one on each side of the forge. At Heathfield, where the first boring mill was located close to the furnace,

46 Sixteenth-century blast furnace (*R. Houghton, after Lucas van Valckenborch*)

1 The Wealden landscape near Frant

2 Siderite iron ore (scale 10cm)

3 *Cyrena* limestone (scale 10cm)

4 Roasted iron ore (scale 10cm)

5 Minepit Wood Late Iron Age/Romano-British bloomery, near Rotherfield (*J. Money*)

6 Little Furnace Wood Romano-British bloomery no.1, near Mayfield

7 Bloomery tap slag from Broadfield; Crawley Museum (scale 10cm)

8 Bloomery slag possibly formed in a slag pit bloomery (scale 10cm)

9 View of Chitcombe Romano-British bloomery site, Brede; the raised area on the far edge of the pale field in the middle of the picture is a slag 'headland' above the stream beyond

10 *Classis Britannica* stamped tile; Battle Museum

11 Guildford Castle; improved using iron from the Weald in 1255

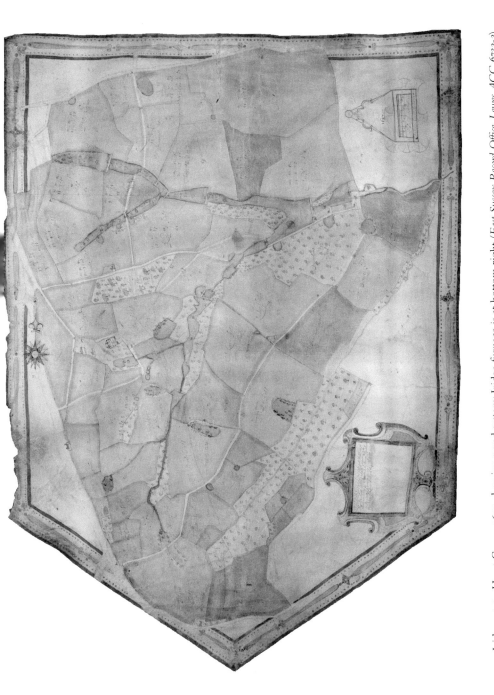

12 Iridge estate, Hurst Green, 1637, showing pond system; Iridge furnace is at bottom right (*East Sussex Record Office, Lewes, ACC 6732-2*)

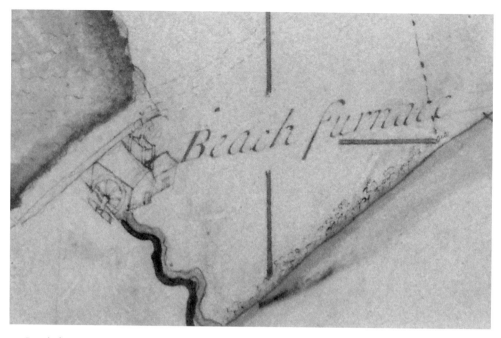

13 Beech furnace, Battle, 1724; detail showing the stack with wooden framework, casting and blowing houses, and waterwheel (*East Sussex Record Office, Lewes, BAT 4421-11*)

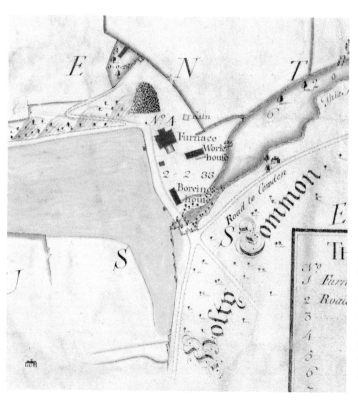

14 Cowden furnace, 1743, detail showing the furnace, workshop and boring mill, as well as a charcoal heap and a kiln, possibly for ore-roasting (*Centre for Kentish Studies, Maidstone, U650-P1*)

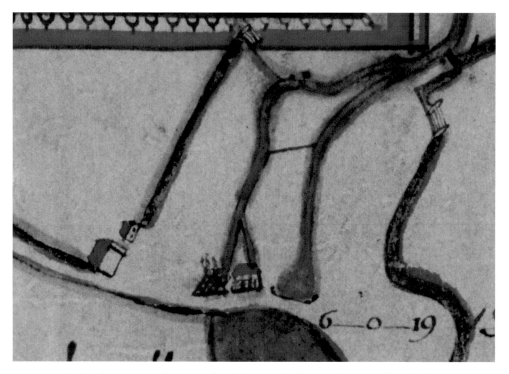

15 Scarlets furnace, Cowden, 1641, detail showing the furnace, boring mill and spillway channels (*East Sussex Record Office, Lewes, ACC 9638-1*)

16 Cast-iron sow, 3.4m long, found at Westfield forge

17 Langleys forge, Maresfield, *c*.1653, detail showing two water wheels and three chimneys (*East Sussex Record Office, Lewes, SAS-AB-17a*)

18 Sir Henry Sidney, owner of Robertsbridge furnace and forge, 1573, by or after Arnold van Brounckhorst (*National Portrait Gallery, London*)

19 Ashburnham furnace; former workshop building

20 Iron slag used as galletting at Dedisham furnace, Rudgwick

21 Gibbshaven, Worth; home of the Thorpe family, ironmasters of Hedgecourt furnace and Woodcock Hammer

22 A Wealden sunken track and ford near Ashburnham

23 Roman iron billet found at Cranbrook (*S. Paynter*)

24 The iron grave slab of Judith Legas, 1747; Wadhurst Church

25 The iron grave slabs of Richard and Mary Still, 1726 and 1730; Cowden churchyard

26 Early seventeenth-century Biblical fireback, showing scenes from the stories of Abraham, Jacob and Joseph; Squerryes Court, Westerham

27 Cast-iron railings around St Paul's Cathedral, London, early eighteenth century

28 Iron stocks and whipping-post at Ninfield

Left: 29 Pippingford furnace excavation, showing the gun-casting pit and pig beds (*D. Meades*)

Below: 30 Inscription on bronze mortar, cast by William Bowen in 1761

a second was built further downstream, and at Ashburnham, the forge was converted to a boring mill, and a second was built later, near to the furnace. When Warren and Gravetye furnaces were both operated by Edward Raby, the boring mill at Warren was used to ream guns from both furnaces. The ones cast at Gravetye were carried by wagon to Warren 'with their heads on'. Other buildings at furnace sites would have included workshops for making moulds, and sheds for the storage of ore and charcoal. These last two were usually situated close to the charging bridge, uphill from the furnace, and patches of ground where the soil has been stained black are often an indication of the location of the coalhouse.

Very few, if any, furnace buildings in the Weald have survived. Unlike the upland areas of Britain, where building stone is more plentiful, no furnace stacks remain standing, even in ruins. Only excavation has revealed their foundations. A probable former working building has survived at Ashburnham, where the present house called 'Furnace' has a culvert beneath it, running its length (*colour plate 19*).

Forges were simpler buildings, being generally rectangular and about 10m wide. They too may have had a coalhouse, and there are references in a number of cases to an 'ironhouse', which was a wholesale warehouse from which blacksmiths and others could purchase bar iron. The stone and brick hearths in the forge, and their chimneys, would probably not have been integral to the structure of the forge building, nor was the massive wooden hammer frame, so when a forge went out of use, it was a relatively simple matter to demolish those elements or remove them. Retaining one of the wheel pits, forge wheels being relatively small in comparison to those used in corn mills, alternative mill machinery could then be installed. While it is unlikely that any of the mills that replaced forges are still housed in the original buildings, the locations may not have changed significantly.

Residential buildings in the Weald have shown a considerable continuity of use, with houses and cottages from the sixteenth century being common and, nowadays, much sought-after. As the majority of workers in the iron industry were also employed seasonally as agricultural labourers, their housing was predominantly tied to farms or estates. With furnaces requiring 24-hour supervision, however, it was essential for the key workers – the founder and the filler and their deputies – to live nearby. For this reason, most furnaces and many forges had one or two cottages in close proximity. Many of these survive. In some instances an ironworks formed the nucleus of a small community, such as at Pounsley, near Framfield, or Darwell, near Mountfield (*47*). At others, perhaps in the remoter locations, like at Hawksden forge, Mayfield, or St Leonard's forge, near Horsham, just a single cottage was built. At Dedisham furnace, near Rudgwick, the furnace cottage was enlarged at about the time the furnace went out of use in the late seventeenth century. Fragments of iron slag were used as galletting in the mortar (*colour plate 20*). This practice, whereby slivers of stone, usually flint, are inserted into the mortar while it is wet, to strengthen it, became more widespread in the following century; this example using slag is rare. Without local shops, the ironworkers were expected to grow some of their own produce, so the cottages usually included closes, or small holdings of land where the ironworkers' families could keep a pig and some chickens, and be able to grow vegetables. The large number of employees at gunfoundries made special housing provision necessary. Groups of cheap cottages were built to house these workers and, in one instance, records survive of a group of smallholdings leased by an ironmaster – in this case, Alexander Master, at Warren furnace, near East Grinstead. Roger's Town, a cluster of cottages on Holtye Common, close to Cowden furnace, may have been established during the second half of the seventeenth century to accommodate artisans working for the Browne family during the time of the Dutch Wars.

It is all too easy to attribute the term, 'ironmaster's house', to almost any fine house in the Weald. However, it is ownership and occupation which defines such places and, in most other respects, they were no different from contemporary houses in the region. Like any other people who had grown wealthy through successful business, ironmasters wanted to display their wealth. The sixteenth century was an age when much rebuilding took place, and the wealth generated by the iron industry manifested itself in some fine houses. As no particular features define an ironmaster's house, nor differentiate

47 Former ironworkers' cottages, Darwell furnace, Mountfield, c.1936 (*J. Mainwaring Baines*)

one from any other mansion or yeoman's residence, the best that can be achieved in these pages is to point to examples. Ironmasters' houses can be divided into three categories: houses which were the homes of individuals before they became ironmasters and which were subsequently enlarged using the profits of their ironworks, houses built by ironmasters from the profits of their ironworks, and houses that ironmasters were able to buy because of their increased wealth and status.

An example of the first is Scotney Castle, near Lamberhurst, which came into the hands of the Darrell family in the early fifteenth century. The Darrells became involved in the iron industry in the 1550s and members of the family had interests in works at Ewood and Leigh in Surrey and at Horsmonden and Chingley in Kent. Scotney was a medieval castle to which the Darrells added a new building, using stone from the ruins of the medieval walls. As the Darrells' fortunes waned with the decline of their iron interests, they sold the property in the mid eighteenth century, and it came into the hands of Edward Hussey, whose grandfather, Thomas, had become wealthy through the ironworks he managed in partnership with John Legas and others, and whose career is detailed above. All that remains are some picturesque ruins overlooked by a more recent house built for Edward Hussey's grandson. Another such property is Tanners at Waldron, which was leased by John Fuller

48 Tanner's, Waldron; home of the Fuller family, ironmasters of Stream furnace

in 1575 (*48*). Eventually purchasing the house and manor, the Fullers did not enter the iron business until 1650. An advantageous marriage settlement which included sugar plantations in Jamaica as much as the wealth accumulated from ironworking, enabled John Fuller's descendant to acquire the more prestigious property of Brightling Place, which he renamed Rose Hill, in 1712.

The Darrells also owned Riverhall, in Wadhurst, the estate spreading across into the neighbouring parish of Frant. In the 1530s they sold it to William Fowle, with whose descendants it remained until the eighteenth century. His son, Nicholas, entered the iron trade and worked the furnace on the property, while another son, Anthony, and his son of the same name, had interests in ironworks in four widely separated parishes. During the eighteenth century Riverhall came into the hands of John Legas, who lived at what is now the Old Vicarage in Wadhurst, and who subsequently built Hill House, both of which are in the High Street. Also in Wadhurst, the Barhams were a major force in the iron industry. Like the Fowles, two branches of the family were involved: those from Shoesmiths, who operated the early forges at Brooklands and Verredge, and who later had an interest in Coushopley furnace; and the Barhams of Scrag Oak furnace, whose house of the same name stands on the hill above the site of the works.

Further to the west, Gravetye, near West Hoathly, was built in 1598 for Richard Infield, who had operated Mill Place furnace. Its association with ironworking in the area was revived in the second half of the eighteenth century when it became the property of William Clutton, whose short-lived attempt to profit from the iron industry, in partnership with James Norden, failed in 1762. The house and the furnace in its grounds were among Clutton's possessions that were put up for sale by his assignees. Like Gravetye, Blackdown House, near Haslemere, on the lower slopes of the hill whose name it bears, was built with the proceeds of iron-making. The Yaldwins, or Yaldens, had been active in the iron industry since the early seventeenth century, leasing Frith furnace and Mitchell Park forge. A date stone on the house, inscribed WY 1640, suggests it was built or altered by William Yaldwin, and the style of the original parts of the house are consistent with that date. Yaldwin was an MP and a fervent supporter of the parliamentary cause in the Civil War, and it is said that Cromwell made the house his headquarters in the area. The proceeds of iron-making did not only find their way into fine country houses. Cromwell House, as it is now called, would have been the finest in East Grinstead when it was built in 1599 for Edward Payne, from the profits of the nearby Stone ironworks (*49*).

Returning to Thomas Hussey, whose descendants were able to purchase Scotney Castle, he also bought himself a fine house. Rampyndene, in Burwash High Street, was built in 1699 for a wool merchant, but Hussey was able to buy it and raise his family there until his death in 1735 (*50*). On a more modest scale is Gibbshaven, near East Grinstead, a timber-framed farmhouse

49 Cromwell House, East Grinstead; built in 1599 by Edward Payne with money made at the nearby Stone ironworks (*East Grinstead Museum*)

50 Rampyndene, Burwash; home, until his death in 1735, of Thomas Hussey, ironmaster at several furnaces and forges

51 Knole, Sevenoaks; rebuilt by Thomas Sackville, Earl of Dorset, owner of ironworks

of the fifteenth century, which was occupied by Richard Thorpe who ran Woodcock Hammer and Hedgecourt furnace (later known as Warren furnace) in the early seventeenth century (*colour plate 21*). It was the Thorpes' growing wealth from ironworking that enabled them to purchase Gibbshaven in 1582, about 15 years after their entry into the iron business. At the other end of the social scale, the mansions of some of the most influential landowners in the Weald, while not necessarily owing their existence to the iron industry, at least reflected the contribution that iron made to the wealth of their estates: places like Knole, at Sevenoaks, the home of the Sackvilles (*51*), Penshurst Place, which belonged to the Sidneys, Petworth House, the seat of the Earls of Northumberland, and Cowdray House, at Midhurst, now a ruin, which was owned by Viscount Montague.

TRANSPORT

The carriage of raw materials and finished products to and from the ironworks was never easy, and the folklore of Sussex has many tales based on the dreadful reputation that the roads had. The geology of the Weald, with its alternating sandstones and clays, created these difficulties. In wet weather, roads across clay were reduced to thick mud with both humans and animals making slow progress, and wheeled vehicles sinking up to their axles; the more so when heavy loads, such as ore or iron, were being carried (*colour plate 22*). So bad were the conditions sometimes that cannon had to be laid up on roadside commons to await drier weather before they could be carried any further. Sussex was one of the last counties where the use of oxen as draught animals was widespread, because only oxen had the strength to make their way in such conditions (*52*). However, the effect on the roads of teams of oxen was to churn up the surface to such an extent that their use by other users was impossible. And it was not only iron that suffered from the problem. Heavy timber for shipbuilding was just as hard, if not harder, to move. Celia Fiennes, writing in the early eighteenth century, noted that it sometimes took as long as two years for a tree trunk to reach Chatham from the Weald; it only being possible to move such heavy loads when it was frosty or dry. Roads across sandstone, while often drier, were more eroded, with many of them forming deeply cut 'hollow ways' with precipitous sides.

   With characteristic thoroughness, the Romans built four major routes across the Weald, three of them serving London. All were properly metalled, and unlike the tracks that were in use for most of the succeeding centuries, did not merely rely on the underlying geology for their basis (*18*). Stane Street linked the capital with Chichester, and posting stations, the modern equivalent of our service areas, were built at Hardham, near Pulborough, and at Alfoldean, just west of Horsham. Although the road does not cross an area

52 Oxen; frequently used to haul heavy loads in the Weald (*Sussex Archaeological Society*)

where evidence of iron smelting has been found, at Alfoldean there is some evidence that ironworking was carried on, perhaps smithing to make and repair metalwork for horses and wagons. Excavations suggested that some of the surface of the road was metalled with iron slag. This practice was much more widely employed on some of the other roads across the region. Further to the east, a road crosses the Weald west of East Grinstead, on the western edge of the area exploited by the Romans. There are a number of sections where slag has been used for metalling. It is not known whether the Romans simply made use of slag that was available within a reasonable distance of the road or whether ironworking sites were established with a view to using the slag to build the road. This road, which links the Stane Street, just south of Southwark, to an east to west road that followed the Greensand ridge north of the South Downs from Lewes to near Chichester, is thought to have been built some time after the occupation had begun. The road that crosses the Weald to the east of East Grinstead passes over Ashdown Forest and also links with the Greensand way near Lewes. Passing through one of the most heavily exploited iron-making areas, its surface is made of slag for a distance of about 30km, requiring a quantity that was equivalent to the output of a substantial and long-standing bloomery site (*53*). Despite the area to the east of this road being much used for iron-making during Roman times, no other main roads have been identified there. A road links the area north of Hastings, where the *Classis Britannica* was active, with the Roman town of Rochester. Passing close to such sites as Footlands, near Sedlescombe, it too is surfaced with slag over part of its route, as is a branch which heads off it

53 Excavations on the
Lewes-London Roman
road at Holtye, 1939
(*Sussex Archaeological
Society*)

near the *Classis* site at Little Farningham Farm, near Cranbrook, and strikes
across the low Weald towards Canterbury. A number of Roman ironworking
sites have been identified in this part of Kent and would, no doubt, have
contributed the slag which was used to surface sections of the route. Near
where this branch road meets yet another Roman road, heading north-west
from the *Classis* port of Lympne, lies the Roman settlement at Westhawk
Farm, south of Ashford. Evidence of iron smelting there shows that it was
probably one of the local crafts that provided metalwork for travellers and
supplied nearby farms. Within this network of major roads must have existed
a mass of smaller tracks giving access from ironworking sites to the main
routes. A few of these have been discovered, such as those in the vicinity
of the *Classis* site at Bardown, near Wadhurst, but many have to be inferred
from surviving lanes and ridgeways. Ironically, when the Victorians began to
do what the Romans had done centuries earlier using ancient slag to surface
their roads, some of the largest Roman ironworking sites in the Weald, such
as Oldlands, near Maresfield, Oaklands, at Sedlescombe, and Chitcombe, near
Brede, were discovered.

We know little of the transportation of iron in the Middle Ages. Pack horse loads were the measure of the amount of ore and charcoal carried to and from the fourteenth-century ironworks at Tudeley. At Horley, in Surrey, in the same century, ore digging took place on the highway, and the perpetrators were fined; it says little for the state of the road that it could be thought to be a suitable place for such work. The rapid increase in the number of ironworks in the sixteenth century led to complaints about the state of the roads as a result of the movement of materials and goods to and from the ironworks. An Act of Parliament was passed in 1584 by which a duty was imposed on ironmasters who had charcoal, iron ore or iron products carried on the public highways between October and May, to either repair the roads with slag or other material or make a monetary payment in lieu. In error, although Surrey and Kent were included in the terms of the Act, Sussex, where most of the ironworks were located, was omitted, and 13 years were to pass before the mistake was put right. The new Act did away with the option to repair the surface during the same period, but imposed a flat rate of three shillings per mile for every three loads of charcoal or ore, or ton of iron, and a duty to repair the roads in the summer months as well. For the time, this legislation seems perfectly reasonable. However, as time went on and ironworks began to be built in other parts of the country, only the Wealden counties continued to be subject to it, placing a financial burden on Wealden ironmasters that was not imposed on those elsewhere. In fact the law was not repealed until 1767, by which time a number of the roads across the Weald had become subject to turnpike acts.

The state of the roads, and the duty payable, placed a premium on moving material in the winter months. However, the need to maintain the cash flow at ironworks made it necessary to move products to their markets even if the majority of the raw materials had been assembled earlier. The high cost of moving products in the winter particularly affected gunfounders in the mid eighteenth century when the Board of Ordnance changed its purchasing arrangements and required orders to be completed by 31 December. Charging a toll on roads where a trust had been set up to repair and maintain them improved the ease of travelling in the Weald, particularly in the wetter times of the year. However, it also added to the cost of moving goods and materials. Turnpike trusts laid down pricing regulations which placed different charges on the number of wheels on wagons, whether they were wide or narrow, and on the number of horses or oxen hauling loads. Ironmasters sometimes found such rules conflicted with the way they could best move their iron. In 1756, Harrison & Co. got into a disagreement with the turnpike trust near Lamberhurst when they were moving guns from the furnace there using a special carriage. It had more wheels than the usual wagon but was of a smaller size, and used more horses. The turnpike trust wanted to charge at a rate based on the number of wheels and horses, but Harrison & Co. claimed they should pay at a rate determined by the size of the wheels, and that their use of the turnpike was in the national interest. It is not recorded how the matter was resolved. Transport overland incurred other charges, notably those of 'trespass'. This was not the illegal entry onto someone else's land as it is now; rather it was a payment made to a landowner to cross his land to make a journey shorter, sometimes to avoid paying a road toll.

The cheapest method of carrying iron was by water. The Romans had appreciated this; access to many of their larger sites in the south-eastern Weald was along the river valleys, then navigable, that flowed into the tidal waters now occupied by Romney Marsh. With at least some of those sites being managed by the *Classis Britannica*, the British Fleet, the option to take iron blooms out of the Weald by sea made good economic sense. What is believed to have been a port was established by the Fleet on the Rother at Bodiam, connected to their sites by a slag-metalled, north to south road. It is not known whether this was the only port the Romans operated, but it seems unlikely, and the Roman pottery and *Classis Britannica* tiles found between Ninfield and Boreham Street, on the edge of the Pevensey Levels, may indicate another such installation.

It is generally reckoned that most Wealden rivers were more navigable, even 250 years ago, than they are now, so there were opportunities for water travel then that might seem inconceivable today. Ralph Hogge's accounts mention iron being taken to Isfield, for transport by barge down the Ouse to Newhaven. In the western Weald, iron from North Park furnace, near Fernhurst, was carried down to the River Arun, en route to Littlehampton. The blast furnaces at Brede and Beckley lay close to navigable stretches of the Brede and Tillingham rivers, and only a short overland journey was necessary before the guns made there could be loaded onto barges and floated down to Rye.

Along the south coast both Hastings and Pevensey were also destinations from furnaces and forges inland. Ironworks in those locations faced a dilemma. With land transport being expensive at any time of the year, and more especially in the wetter seasons, should the products be taken by the shorter, overland route, or was it worth making the land journey to the nearest river followed by longer but cheaper water transport? Often, the conditions at the time dictated the method used. In wartime, coastal shipping could be subject to attack. Fast enemy vessels would be stationed off the Channel ports, ready to swoop on the slow transport ships, or hoys, carrying the iron. In the eighteenth century, the demand for guns was sufficient for the navy to organise convoys to give the merchant ships some protection. The sea journey along the south coast and into the North Sea brought shipping perilously close to the shore of France or the Spanish possessions in the Netherlands, with winds and tides sometimes making it difficult to steer close to the English coast. One advantageous route open to furnaces and forges in the northern part of the Weald was along the Medway, which became tidal near

54 Branbridges, East Peckham; access point to the River Medway for iron from the Wealden furnaces and forges (*Centre for Kentish Studies, Maidstone, EAP 5*)

Maidstone and flowed into the Thames estuary. Hoys carrying iron had only a short voyage up the Thames to London. Like all rivers, however, the Medway contained shallows and bends that caused barges difficulty, so in the second quarter of the eighteenth century several Wealden ironmasters were among those who began to lobby for improvements to be made to the river. In 1740 the Medway Navigation enabled barges to take on goods at Branbridges, near East Peckham, and shallower vessels could be loaded as far up as Tonbridge (*54*). John Fuller, who was closer to Newhaven, and the Crowleys at Ashburnham, which was only a few miles from Hastings, sometimes sent their guns overland to the Medway rather than run the risk of losing their precious cargoes.

7

PRODUCTS

From the pre-Roman Iron Age until the end of the Middle Ages, the product of the bloomery furnace was a bloom. When it had undergone initial consolidation after being withdrawn from the furnace, it would have been formed into a billet or a bar. The only examples of such objects discovered in the Weald are those found at the *Classis Britannica* site at Little Farningham Farm, Cranbrook (*colour plate 23*), and at Westhawk Farm. near Ashford. The Cranbrook billet was probably forged from only part of a bloom, the original having been split, perhaps prior to further forging. A distinctive form of iron that would have been forged from blooms, and noted in other parts of the country, although no examples have been found in the Weald, has been referred to as a currency bar. While not of uniform size, these are likely to represent a marketable form of bloomery iron and probably had a recognisable value for trading purposes. The Cranbrook bloom could have been forged into such a shape. Once the bloom had been hammered into a saleable form, it would be down to the skill of the smith to make it into a useable implement. Reliable analysis of wrought iron artefacts using the characteristics of slag trapped in the metal to gauge their origin is not yet available, but such was the output of the larger ironworks in the Roman period, particularly some of those in the south-eastern part of the region, that iron artefacts with a Wealden origin might be expected to be found in other parts of Britain.

The process during the Saxon and medieval periods was the same as in Roman times, although the markets would have been different in some respects. We know from the accounts of the ironworks at Tudeley in the fourteenth century that blooms were being made, although we have no data on their size. We know that forging of those blooms was not undertaken where they were smelted, and can only assume that the bloom was the marketable form. Blooms are recorded as the product of other ironworks in the same period. Ralph Kenne, who made iron in Wartling manor at the beginning of the fourteenth century, had to surrender a bloom to the lord of the manor in payment for the right to continue to operate his works. The value of his bloom, at 2s 6d, was half as much again as those at Tudeley 20 years later. The Tudeley blooms were sometimes split; this was either to give evidence of their quality, or to allow smaller quantities to be sold. We have no evidence of the size of Wealden blooms in the Middle Ages. A weight of 30lb (13kg) has been suggested, based on bloom sizes from other regions, but it is more likely they were smaller. Smiths in and beyond the Weald would have worked up the blooms produced there, turning them into as wide a range of tools, implements and utensils as their Roman predecessors. Among these, the most important seem to have been horseshoes and nails, of which large quantities were being purchased in the Weald in the thirteenth and fourteenth centuries, particularly from the Archbishop of Canterbury's estates. Horseshoe-making is also mentioned at Roffey, near Horsham in the fourteenth century, as are arrows – both the shafts and the heads. However, the relatively small scale of the iron which they had to work with meant that smiths wanting to make larger pieces of ironwork had to weld pieces together, which was expensive and time-consuming. As well as this functional use of iron, examples of which are generally rare because they were discarded when worn out or broken, some decorative use of iron has survived. As with objects from the Roman period, it is difficult to be sure where a piece of iron has been made, but examples found in the Weald are unlikely to have been the products of other regions. The decorative hinges and other ironwork on the church door at Staplehurst, in Kent, are such a case (55). Reckoned to date from the eleventh century, our knowledge of ironworking sites at that time offers no suggestion as to where they may have been made.

The substantial increase in the output of blast furnaces and their finery forges, compared with bloomeries, meant that iron became much more widely available and on a larger scale. Instead of a single-stage process, two stages had to be gone through to produce the wrought iron needed by smiths, but a sow of cast iron weighing up to 500kg could be made into several bars of wrought iron, each as much as 3m long, and two sows might be cast each day. Sows were unwieldy objects, perhaps as their name suggests, and manoeuvring them from the bed of sand in front of the furnace where they had been cast, onto a wagon and then off again at the forge, before feeding them through the aperture in the side of the finery hearth, was difficult and laborious. In time, sows were made smaller and more manageable. Also, as the capacity of furnace hearths increased, it became possible to cast more than one sow at a time, or to cast smaller ingots of iron, which became known as pigs. The latter were more useful for remelting in reverberatory, or air, furnaces, which began to be constructed in urban locations from the seventeenth century onwards. As with the Middle Ages and earlier, once the cast iron had been converted to wrought iron in the finery, the potential variety of products was only

55 Medieval ironwork on the door of Staplehurst Church, *circa* eleventh century

dependent on the skill and imagination of the blacksmith. With the basis of their work being a long iron bar, the range for single-forged articles became greater. Agricultural tools such as plough shares, building materials such as nails, domestic articles like hearth implements, and vehicle accessories like wheel tyres were all within the scope of the smith's output. In the Goudhurst area, some smiths seem to have specialised in the manufacture of edged tools in the sixteenth century. At Gulledge, a sixteenth-century timber-framed house near East Grinstead, the addition of a stone frontage, probably at the beginning of the 1600s, was supported by two, long, wrought-iron straps which secured the stonework to the original wooden frame. Iron wire was a specialised manufacture; a wire mill set up at Chilworth, in Surrey, south-east of Guildford, in 1603 was a short-lived venture. Wire-making required iron forged to a special quality, known as Osmund iron. A brief reference to 'osbourne' iron in the accounts of Robertsbridge furnace in the first part of the eighteenth century may indicate such work there. Nail-making was also specialised work, and became a cottage industry in the Midlands. Although smiths in the Weald would have been able to forge large nails for heavy construction work, the only reference to nails being made was at Sheffield forge. Examples of other forgings have been found at excavated fineries at Chingley, Ardingly and Blackwater Green, where iron wedges figure prominently. Finds of small pieces of domestic ironware, such as scissors and locks, are more likely to have been discarded possessions than manufactured at the sites. Fineries also produced large, specialised pieces of ironwork, such as boring bars for gunfoundries. These required replaceable steel cutting edges that removed the rough iron from the barrels of cannon. Although at least four steel forges have been noted in the Weald, no indication as to other uses for the steel, apart from being sold to merchants in London and elsewhere, has been recorded.

What the blast furnace was capable of producing that had not been available from the bloomery were products made of cast iron formed in moulds. Casting objects made of other metals, such as bronze, had been understood since pre-historic times, but in Europe the use of iron for casting had only been possible once liquid iron had been deliberately made in the blast furnace. Even then,

56 Cross and inscription on the graveslab of John Collins, c.1537; Burwash Church

the considerably higher temperature of molten iron (1500°C), compared with bronze (900°C), caused problems when finding suitable materials into which the iron could be poured. Cast items were among the first things made at Newbridge furnace after it was built in 1496, and these included cannon balls, which were to become an important and relatively easily made product of Wealden furnaces. For quite a long time, however, castings did not figure largely in the output of the furnaces in the region; the most important trade being in bar iron forged from cast sows.

Among the oldest surviving castings are iron memorials or grave slabs. Simple to produce because of their rectangular shape, one in Burwash Church is believed to be the earliest. This largely plain plate bears a small floriated cross, beneath which are the words '*ORATE P ANNEMA JHONE COLINE*' – 'Pray for the soul of John Collins' (56). The plate was made by preparing a flat bed of damp sand with raised edges. Nearer one end the impression of a cross was made by pushing just such an object into the sand and then removing it. The words were probably carved onto a small piece of wood, which was then similarly pressed into the sand. When the iron was poured onto the sand the cross and letters were raised in relief. Early writers on the iron industry assumed that the Lombardic style of lettering used, which was popular in the thirteenth and fourteenth centuries, indicated that the memorial dated from that period, but as the use of cast iron was only introduced with the blast furnace in the 1490s it could not date from before then. Also, the phrase, '*orate pro anima*' commonly appears on memorials from the 1450s onwards. It is almost certainly a memorial to the John Collins who operated Socknersh furnace and who died in 1537. Nearly 90 of these memorials can be seen in the Weald, mostly inside churches. A few are in churchyards, either as headstones or on altar tombs, and at least two, although undoubtedly made in the Weald, lie in churches beyond its borders, at Bermondsey in south-east London, and at Rivenhall in Essex. The largest number is in Wadhurst Church, where there are 33. The earliest dated memorial

57 Anne Barcley's graveslab, 1570; East Grinstead Church

commemorates Anne Barcley, who died in 1570 (57). Hers is one of three iron memorials in East Grinstead, the others dating from 1616 and 1714. Most of those buried under iron had some connection with families involved in the iron trade and such connections are sometimes indicated by similarities between memorials. Gabriel Egles, whose plate is the only one made of iron in Uckfield Church, was related to the Barhams, many of whom are commemorated by plates in Wadhurst. One group of memorials shows clearly that they were the products of the same furnace and founder. All dating from between 1653 and 1667, seven plates commemorate eight people from five families buried in four churches. Their inscriptions all include the phrase '*aetatis suae*' – 'of his age' (58). The phrase was common on Tudor portraits, indicating the age of the sitter. On three of the plates, however, the phrase is followed by the year of death, not the age of the deceased, suggesting that the person charged with impressing the inscription, using individual letters from a stock alphabet, was none too literate. On all of them, 'aetatis' is spelt 'aeatis'; on all except two the missing 't' is added above. Finally, on two of the plates, the founder has placed his own initials – 'T.C.'

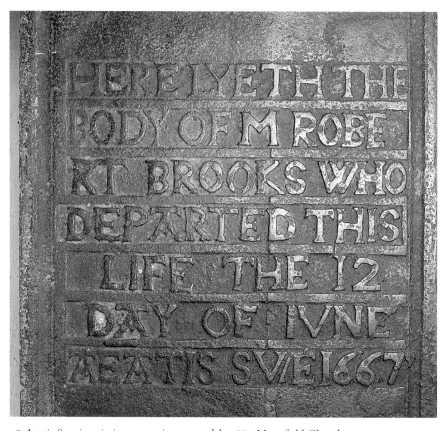

58 Aetatis Suae inscription on an iron graveslab, 1667; Maresfield Church

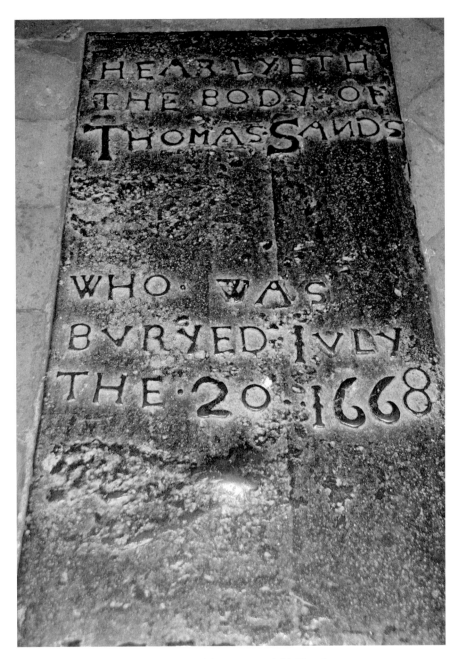

59 Rough casting: Thomas Sands' graveslab, 1668; Mayfield Church

The quality of the castings varies enormously, but apparently not according to age. The memorial to Thomas Sands, who died in 1668 and who was buried in the aisle of Mayfield Church, has reversed letters in crooked lines, and with imperfections in the casting that indicate that the iron was poured carelessly onto the bed of sand (59). Reversed letters on inscriptions were common in an age when the majority of the workforce was illiterate. The poor quality of this slab is highlighted even more by the fine state of the adjacent plate, to Sands' grandson, also Thomas, who died in 1708 (60). His memorial bears the arms of the Coopers' Company, of which he was a member, as well as incised lettering (not without errors) and an incised floral decoration below. The arms would have been carved on a wooden board, perhaps lent by the Company rather than made specially, which would then have been impressed on the sand. In a few instances, the iron plate serves merely as a background for the inscription in another metal. Agnes Faulconer's death at West Hoathly in 1635 is remembered on a brass plate fixed to a plain iron slab (61), as is the memorial to Martha, the wife of John Browne, the gunfounder, buried at Horsmonden in 1644. The grave slab over the tomb of Judith, wife of John Legas, in Wadhurst Church, is an uncommonly smooth, plain, iron plate with the letters 'J.L.' and the date '1747' inlaid in brass – elegant simplicity (*colour plate 24*). In contrast, some memorials include in the inscriptions as much information as possible. The plate commemorating Martha, the wife of the gunfounder Peter Gott, and three of their children, was not installed in Streat Church, north-west of Lewes until at least 1754. However, the details of the eight children on the memorial suggest that the pattern for the plate had been prepared in the 1730s, with the date of Elizabeth Gott's death added before it was cast about 20 years later. Similarly detailed is the memorial to Martha Gott's father, Thomas Western, dated 1703, at Rivenhall, near Witham in Essex.

Equally varied are the memorials outside churches. Some, like that of Elizabeth Playstead of Wadhurst, whose memorial, dated 1799, was the last to be made in the Weald, are simply cast. Others are more complicated. The graves of Richard and Mary Still, in Cowden churchyard, have iron plates that could not have been cast in simple sand moulds (*colour plate 25*). Their overhanging edges could only have been made in closed box moulds; a sophistication not seen elsewhere in the region. Most, if not all, iron memorials were made to order. However, rare survivals are two iron headstones in the porch of Brightling Church, which have never been used. Now badly corroded, it is still possible to see, by their length, that they were intended to be buried deeply in the soil. Others of an identical pattern have already been used in the churchyard, some with barely decipherable incised inscriptions dating from the mid eighteenth century (62). Additions to church buildings or alterations to churchyards have sometimes resulted in graves being moved. Usually they have been relocated into the church, but occasionally memorials have been found far from their original resting place, such as the memorial to Robert

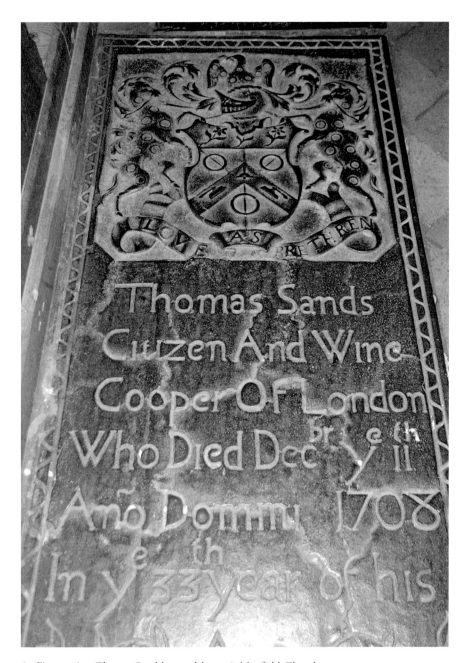

60 Fine casting: Thomas Sands' graveslab, 1708; Mayfield Church

61 Brass on iron: Agnes Faulconer's graveslab, 1635; West Hoathly Church

Bakar of Withyham, part of whose memorial of 1585 is in Anne of Cleves Museum, Lewes, or the plate which probably commemorates a child or children of the Fowle family, now in Maidstone Museum.

Among the most commonly seen pieces of Wealden ironwork are firebacks. The change from the domestic practice of having the fireplace on the floor of the open hall of a house, to the construction of a smoke-bay or a brick chimney, coincided with the growth of iron casting. It was natural that once iron became more widely available it should be used for the three-fold purpose of protecting the back of fireplaces, providing a means of reflecting the heat into rooms, and forming a decorative, even personalised, object of domestic pride. To begin with, firebacks were often plain with simple designs formed from easily available objects, such as carved wood derived from furniture, pieces of rope or even domestic implements. It was soon realised that with a stock of prepared patterns, including letters of the alphabet and heraldic charges, founders could cast firebacks with designs tailored to the wishes of the purchaser. The use and variety of these movable patterns, as well as their occurrence in defined groups, suggests that certain patterns were used by particular furnaces. One group, comprising heraldic lions, shields and other patterns with royal associations can be observed with many combinations of the patterns (63). Similarly, another group includes patterns of wooden strips with trailing vines, birds and *rose en soleil* motifs. This particular group is associated with a fireback bearing the arms of Edward VI, on which is the inscription 'Made in Sussex by John Harvo'. Harvo was a known gunfounder, probably of immigrant origin, who supplied the Crown and operated Pounsley furnace, near Framfield, in the 1550s. It seems probable that the stock of patterns used to make the firebacks on which they were cast were also from Pounsley. The same pattern, formed from a wooden strip with trailing vine leaf design, is found on several examples of a rare but distinctive group of firebacks, all of which, unusually, bear the same memorial inscription:

HER:LIETH:ANE:FORST
R:DAVGHTER:AND:
HEYR:TO:THOMAS:
GAYNSFORD:ESQVIER
DECEASED:XVIII:OF:
IANVARI:1591:LEAVYNG
BEHIND:HER:II:SONES:
AND:V:DAVGHTERS

The inscription is identical to one on an iron memorial in Crowhurst Church, Surrey. At least six versions of the fireback are known, all different, but with the inscription in common (64). Many have the vine leaf pattern and one very large example, which was formerly at Baynard's Park, Surrey, had the

62 Inscribed iron headstone, 1744; Brightling churchyard

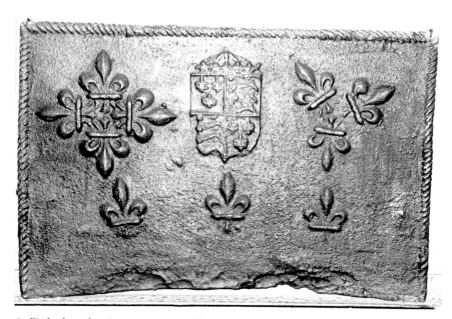

63 Fireback made using separate moveable stamps, mid sixteenth century

64 Fireback with 'Anne Forster' inscription, *c*.1591; East Grinstead Church

inscription used twice. It is a little difficult, by twenty-first-century standards, to understand how it might be acceptable to have someone's memorial ever present at the back of one's fireplace. The most likely reason for the different versions being cast lies in the inscription itself, where it is clearly stated that Anne Forster was Thomas Gaynsford's heir and, by implication, so were her sons and daughters. Perhaps the firebacks were cast to assert their claim to their grandfather's estate. Uncharitably, it could also be suggested that an unscrupulous iron founder, having cast the original grave slab, made use of the carved pattern bearing the inscription to make some money by casting firebacks. His clientele, being largely illiterate, would have been unaware of its significance and unlikely to take offence.

Using entire wooden patterns, it was possible to decorate firebacks with prepared designs; these would have benefited from a greater degree of care than the designs formed from sometimes haphazardly arranged stamps and objects. Initially, patterns covering the whole fireback were carved with coats of arms, often royal, but sometimes personal, and some bearing the arms of London livery companies. Biblical scenes were rarely portrayed on firebacks in the Weald, perhaps because of the growth of radical Protestantism which was opposed to graven images. However, a group of firebacks, thought to have been cast at Brede furnace, includes a small number with religious subjects. One remarkable example at Squerryes Court, near Westerham, illustrates no less than three Old Testament scenes drawn from the Book of Genesis (*colour plate 26*). Many firebacks bear little more than a date and a set of initials. Giles Moore, the rector of Horsted

Keynes, recorded in his diary that in 1657 he had a fireback cast at the local furnace bearing the initials of himself and his wife, which cost him 13s. The next year he bought another, this time with the arms of a local family, the Michelbornes, on it. It only cost 10s, probably because the furnace kept the wooden pattern in stock and they did a small trade in off-the-shelf firebacks with that design.

From the mid seventeenth century onwards, following the Restoration of Charles II and more particularly following the accession of William III in 1688, a new style of fireback became increasingly popular. Since the introduction of firebacks in the mid sixteenth century their size and shape had been dictated by the fireplaces that they were cast for. By the closing years of the Stuart period, house design had resulted in smaller fireplaces which were no longer able to accommodate the wide firebacks made formerly. The 'Dutch' style of fireback, so named because many of them came from North Germany via the Netherlands, were typified by a rather uniform shape, with a pictorial scene surrounded by floral decoration, and often surmounted by fish or serpents. The pictorial element included Biblical and Classical scenes. Also popular were iconic figures representing Charity, Fortune and other subjects. The interchangeability of the pictorial scenes and the borders has suggested that patterns for each were separate and could be tailored to the purchaser's own requirements. Although many of these continental firebacks were used as patterns for subsequent copies, some Wealden founders made examples in a similar style using locally carved patterns. A group of such firebacks was produced at Ashburnham furnace at the very end of iron smelting in the region (65).

Associated with firebacks were andirons, or firedogs (66). These pieces of cast iron were made to support the logs in a domestic fireplace. They were assembled from two parts; a plain, L-shaped casting was made first, and when that was cold it was suspended above an open sand mould formed from a decorative, two-legged pattern. As the molten iron was poured into the mould, the suspended part became firmly married to the front end. The upper parts of firedogs were sometimes decorated with figures; their two-legged form giving them an animated quality. They could also have shields, symbols or initials cast on them to personalise them.

The iron industry itself provided a market for some cast goods. Hammers and anvils and hearth plates for finery forges were made at Heathfield. Other cast ironware made at Wealden furnaces included rollers. Most of these were for domestic gardens, but the Fullers at Heathfield furnace made sugar rollers for the plantations they owned in Jamaica. Trucks – the metal wheels for gun carriages – were made at a few furnaces, especially during wartime, as were cannon balls, or round shot. These were made

Right: 65 English fireback copying the 'Dutch' style, made at Ashburnham, early nineteenth century

Below: 66 Cast-iron firedogs, *circa* sixteenth century; East Court, East Grinstead

67 Cast-iron shot mould from Glazier's forge; bottom half (scale 10cm)

in huge numbers, with examples still being dug up near furnaces today. They were cast in reusable metal moulds, with the iron ladled from the forehearth of the furnace (67). A few ironworks, where the founder was particularly skilled, were able to produce shells. In effect hollow cannon balls, these were made to be fired from mortars and howitzers, and were packed with gunpowder, with a fuse protruding from a hole. Iron railings were generally made by blacksmiths, but when, in 1710, the Dean and Chapter of the new St Paul's Cathedral, in London, decided to erect a 'fence', as they described it, to enclose the church (contrary to the wishes of Sir Christopher Wren, the architect), an order was placed for an elaborate cast-iron structure (colour plate 27). The contractor was Richard Jones, an ironmonger, but the work was carried out by Samuel Gott at the Gloucester furnace, Lamberhurst. Rumours abound to this day that some of the casting was sub-contracted to other furnaces, but there is no evidence to support this. The whole contract cost over £11,000 (more than a million pounds in modern money). Much of this is due to the fact that there were over 11,000 components, and that they incorporated a combination of wrought and cast iron, as well as threaded elements. The St Paul's railings may well have been one of the most sophisticated pieces of cast ironwork of their time. Perhaps one of the more unusual pieces of ironwork are the stocks and whipping-post at Ninfield (colour plate 28). Unique in the Weald, they are a combination of wrought and cast iron.

GUNFOUNDING

Early iron guns were made of wrought iron. Using hoops and bars of iron, these weapons were constructed in much the same way as barrels, hence the name of the firing tube. Separate chambers for the gunpowder were also made of wrought iron, using a technique whereby, at sufficient temperature, the iron bars or plates can be welded together by hammering. As molten iron was not necessary in the construction of these guns, their introduction preceded the development of the blast furnace and they were in use by the mid fourteenth century. Most were relatively small because of the limited size of the iron bars produced by the bloomery method. When the blast furnace was introduced, bar iron on a larger scale became available and construction of bigger guns became possible. Guns of this sort were recovered from the wreck of the *Mary Rose*, sunk in 1543 in Portsmouth Harbour. Another example of a similar type of gun stood at Eridge, south of Tunbridge Wells, until the late eighteenth century. It was rediscovered in Suffolk in the 1970s and is now in the collection of the Royal Armouries. Although it is possible that these guns could have been made using iron from the Weald, there is no direct evidence that they were. The alternative was guns made of cast bronze. Their production developed from bell founding and, by the end of the fifteenth century, continental founders were making cannon in a form which was not to change radically for the next 400 years.

Casting guns in iron had been among the earliest activities at Newbridge furnace, but in the early days, the weapons they had made had been small, two-piece affairs. Cast-iron cannon had been made in Italy, but had not been accepted widely because of their unreliability. It took a political crisis of international importance to provide the trigger for a technological advance that was to place the Weald in the forefront of European expansion. 'The king's great matter' – the divorce of Henry VIII from Catherine of Aragon – sparked off an international row which placed England at risk of invasion by several of her continental neighbours. Henry put into action a major building programme that established a chain of castles and smaller forts around the south coast of England. Pride in his navy had caused the king to commission the brass ordnance he had needed to equip his vessels from the leading continental founders. As early as the second decade of the sixteenth century Henry had encouraged some of the founders to come to London and set up their foundries there, but this did not significantly reduce the cost of such weapons, the price of copper and tin from sources in the kingdom being high. Such an ambitious programme of military expansion drew heavily on the royal purse – a cheaper alternative needed to be found and in 1543 the novel collaboration between the French gunfounder, Peter Baude, and the English iron-maker, Ralph Hogge, resulted in the successful casting of an iron cannon at Buxted in Sussex.

In fact, the casting of iron cannon was one of the most technically demanding industrial processes of the period. Other forms of casting required more precise skills, such as the production of statuary, but with iron guns, where the products were cast directly from the furnace in which the iron was smelted, there was an additional requirement – that of speed of working. For in the typical gunfoundry of the sixteenth, seventeenth or eighteenth centuries, there was the pressure of demand, particularly in wartime, the necessity of continual casting (because the furnace could not be allowed to go out) and the fact that the majority of the work could only take place in the winter when the furnaces were active. A veritable production line had to be maintained to ensure that orders were completed on time and that there was no wastage. A further complication was that each gun had its own individual mould, which could not be reused.

To make the mould, you started with a tapered wooden spindle, somewhat longer than the cannon would be. Around this spindle, rope was tightly wound and fixed temporarily at both ends. Then, using the rope as a key, the moulders would build up an exact model of the gun in clay. The shape was determined by rotating the model against a wooden template, called a strickle board, into which the precise positions and shapes of the various reinforcing rings had been cut. The model would have to be made slightly larger than the gun would turn out to be because of the shrinkage of the iron when it cooled. An extraneous part of the model was formed in front of the gun's muzzle, the purpose of which will be explained in due course. The trunnions – the protrusions on each side of the gun on which it was pivoted in its carriage – and any decoration, such as a royal cipher, were then added (68). The whole model would then be baked hard. When that was completed, the model was covered with a layer of wax or fat and then several coats of liquid clay slurry were painted over the model before stiffer clay, mixed with hair, was added to a thickness of about 10cm. The mould itself was now being formed. When this was done and the clay baked hard, the whole mould was encased in a framework of metal straps. The rope which had been wrapped around the spindle was then detached, and with a sharp blow from a mallet the spindle was dislodged and pulled out from the inside of the model. The rope, which was stuck to the inside of the model, was then slowly pulled out and, with it, the pieces of the model, which broke away from the mould, the wax or fat allowing the model to be removed without damaging the mould that had been formed around it. The inside of the mould would then be inspected for blemishes, and the wooden trunnion models removed, before a fire was set in the void to bake the clay and melt any remaining wax or fat.

The mould would, at this stage, be open at both ends, so when it was brought to the casting pit, or vault, in front of the furnace, it would have to be lowered carefully onto a separate mould of the breech end of the gun, which is known as the cascable. At Pippingford furnace an adjustable table was found in the

68 Making a cannon model (*from Diderot & Alembert, Encyclopédie, 1751-72*)

casting vault, allowing guns of different lengths to be cast (*69*). Finally, the core had to be made and placed into position. This was necessary so that the gun would be cast with a barrel. Making the core was similar to making the model of the cannon itself. This time, a metal bar, called the nowell bar, was wrapped in rope and clay was built over it so that its diameter almost matched the intended calibre of the gun. The core was then lowered carefully into the void inside the cannon mould and positioned centrally using two metal rings, with spikes protruding from each, called crowns, one crown at each end of the core, which would rest against the inside of the mould. These would be lost into the casting. All would then be ready for the molten iron to be poured in. The two biggest sources of failure when casting guns were either dampness in the mould, because of insufficient drying, or the dislodging of the core by the downward flow of molten iron. The former would result in the iron breaking through the mould, often violently, while the latter would cause the barrel to be misaligned and the walls of the barrel to be of uneven thickness. If all went well and the pouring of the metal, which of course was just as heavy when liquid as it was when solid, had not caused either of the problems just mentioned, the casting would be allowed to cool slowly. Slow cooling was essential to cause the carbon in the cast iron to take the form of graphite, which would give the iron greater resilience and make finishing the iron, by sawing and filing, easier. Next, the nowell bar was removed along with the rope that was wrapped round it, and with the latter, the pieces of the clay core. Then the metal strapping was undone and put aside for reuse, and the

69 Gun-casting table construction (scale 30cm) (*R. Houghton*)

mould itself was broken, to free it from the gun inside. Finally, the gunhead, the extraneous part of the casting referred to earlier, into which impurities and gas bubbles would rise during pouring, would be sawn off, any external blemishes filed away, and the cannon would be sent to the boring mill for the rough inside of the barrel to be reamed to the correct diameter.

Since, until the 1770s, cannon were cast with a core, it was only necessary to remove unevenness along the gun barrel and ensure that its diameter was correct for the shot it was expected to discharge. On the continent, gun boring was carried out on a vertical rig probably powered by a horse. However, remains of a trolley found at Pippingford indicate that in the Weald the barrels were smoothed out, or reamed, using a horizontal apparatus powered by water (70). A reconstruction of a boring mill, using a seventeenth-century boring bar found at Stream furnace, Chiddingly, is on display at Anne of Cleves House Museum, Lewes.

The entire gunfounding process had to be undergone for every gun that was made; it not being possible to reuse the moulds. When one considers that, by the end of the seventeenth century, some Wealden furnaces would be able to produce more than 100 guns in as little as, or less than, six months, and sometimes cast as many as three guns at a time, one can appreciate the extraordinary achievement of the gunfoundry workforce. In the sixteenth and seventeenth centuries, guns had fanciful names, such a saker, minion, falcon and culverin, but later these were abandoned and more prosaic descriptions applied instead. The smallest made in the Weald fired a shot weighing half a pound (0.22kg) (71). These were often referred to as swivel guns because they were usually fixed into U-shaped swivelling mountings on the deck rails of ships. The next sizes – 1-, 2-, 3-, 4-, 6-, 9- and 12-pounders – were often found on merchant vessels. They varied in length; the longer the barrel, the greater the range. The great guns – 18, 24 and 32 pounders – were only found on naval ships, and only certain furnaces were capable of casting them because of the need to have a deep enough casting vault; a 32 pounder weighed 2¾ tons and was 9½ft (2.9m) long in its finished state (72). In the mould it was probably 18in (0.5m) longer because of the gunhead. The adjustable table at Pippingford (*colour plate 29*) would have enabled the founder to increase or decrease the depth of the pit to accommodate different lengths of gun mould. An even larger gun, the Cannon of 7, or 42-pounder, was cast in small numbers by George and John Browne, and by Thomas Western, in the 1670s. In their finished state these guns weighed almost three tons and posed considerable problems in casting. The limited capacity of Wealden furnace hearths meant that it was only possible to cast such guns when the walls of the hearth had been eroded by several months of use. Even then, it was necessary to retain the molten iron in the hearth for as much as four days to accumulate enough to fill the mould of one of these guns at a single attempt. Not only was there a danger of the molten iron breaking through the walls

70 Cannon-boring bar, seventeenth century, found at Stream furnace (*D. Butler*)

71 Half-pounder swivel gun, eighteenth century

72 32-pounder demi-cannon, *c.*1760s, made at Ashburnham (*C. Trollope*)

of the hearth, but also of the temperature of the iron dropping to the point where it would not pour.

As has already been noted, in the 1630s John Browne started casting guns in bronze as well as iron, and in the eighteenth century William Bowen and Edward Raby did also. Bronze metal in the form of ingots or captured cannon was sent by the Board of Ordnance to their gunfoundries for remelting in air furnaces. Mortars and howitzers were made of bronze (*colour plate 30*). Due to the fine quality of the metal, it was easy for bronze founders to embellish their guns with elaborate designs and inscriptions, such as the coats of arms of their patrons and the name of the founder. With iron cannon, this was not as easy to do. The earliest cast iron guns rarely bore any markings at all. As many of the guns were being purchased by the Crown, some insignia was felt to be necessary to identify them, so a royal badge, consisting of a rose surmounted by a crown, was cast onto these guns. From the reign of George II onwards, this was replaced by a crowned cipher. Sometimes the ironmaster would have his initials chiselled into the metal as well. However, a uniform marking system took time to become established. The fact that their moulds were not reusable made it rare for any two guns in a batch to be of the same weight, so this was used for identification and the figures, in hundredweights, quarters and pounds, were chiselled into the metal at the rear of the gun. A practice that developed in Sweden, to identify the guns made at different furnaces involved casting a letter, or letters, onto one or both of the gun's trunnions. This practice began to be adopted in England from the end of the seventeenth century, so guns cast at Wealden furnaces in the eighteenth century can be identified as follows (*73*):

Table 1 The letters cast into guns to identify their ironmaster and furnace

Left trunnion	Right trunnion	Ironmaster	Furnace
	A		Ashburnham
	B		Brede
	C		Conster (Beckley)
	CM	Charles Manning	Pippingford
	D		Darwell (Mountfield)
	G		Gloucester (Lamberhurst)
	H		Hamsell (Rotherfield)
	IB	James Bourne	Robertsbridge
	IF	John Fuller (1693–1722 & 1745–55)	Heathfield
JC	D or R	John Churchill	Darwell or Robertsbridge
	JF	John Fuller (1722–45)	Heathfield
	MR	Master & Raby	Warren (Worth)
	R		Robertsbridge
	RF	Rose Fuller	Heathfield
	WB	William Bowen	Barden or Cowden
	W		Waldron

73 Ashburnham trunnion mark, seventeenth century

Gunfounding was a pressurised business. In wartime, in particular, the requirement to complete orders, combined with the need to prepare a steady stream of gun moulds, properly dried to avoid failures during casting, usually at the time of year when the worst weather could be expected, were made worthwhile by the high profits. It never formed the main business of more than 12 to 15 furnaces at any one time but, as the demand for bar iron from forges diminished, that number accounted for an increasing proportion of the furnaces working in the Weald until, during the middle decades of the eighteenth century, it became the main business of the ironworks in the region. Their products are still to be found all over the world, as far afield as Barbados and the Australian coast, wherever the British navy or British mercantile interests were engaged.

APPENDIX 1

WHERE TO SEE WEALDEN IRON

With the three exceptions that follow, the sites where iron was made in the Weald lie on private land. Public footpaths offer the curious the opportunity to pass through some sites; please see Appendix 2 for details.

Ebernoe furnace, Kirdford, West Sussex, SU 9751 2770 (74)
This furnace was owned by the Smythe family and was probably worked in conjunction with their forge at Wassell, nearby. They bought the Wassell estate in 1594. The furnace is mentioned in an account related to charcoal burning in 1610. It probably did not operate for very long, if the remains are anything to go by.

   The pond is in water. The bay is nearly 100m long and 3m high on the downstream side. The modern spillway at the south end of the bay may be where the original spillway was situated. Remains of an outlet near the middle of the bay indicate the probable position of the former sluice, together with the site of the furnace. Some glassy slag can be found near this channel.

Crowborough Warren furnace, Withyham, East Sussex, TQ 4960 3220
In the lists of 1574, John Baker, of Battle, is noted as the occupier of a furnace and forge in Withyham. No other history is known. The forge, anciently known as Grubsbars, lies about 0.5km downstream.

   The pond is dry. The bay is about 115m long and a little over 5m high on the downstream side. It is breached by the stream at its eastern end, where it passes under a later packhorse bridge. This breach probably coincides with the position of the former sluice. The spillway was at the western end of the bay, where a banked channel extends for over 60m, to avoid water getting onto the former working area. About 35m downstream of the packhorse bridge, large blocks of stone in a tree root next to the stream probably

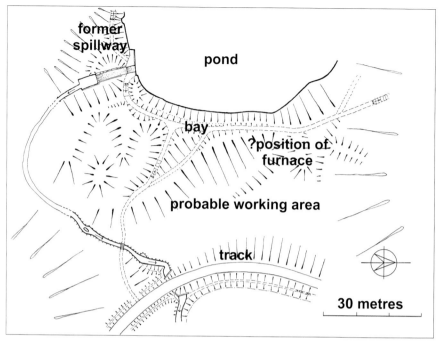

74 Ebernoe furnace plan (*R. Houghton*)

indicate the position of the furnace. Further downstream are extensive heaps of glassy slag.

Newbridge furnace and forge, Hartfield, East Sussex, TQ 4557 3248 (75)
Built in 1496, it was set up by Henry Fyner, a goldsmith, but occupied initially by Peter Roberts. He was replaced by Pauncelett Symart in 1498. Initial work was for the construction of gun carriages, but other early products include iron shot as well as sows. Later there are references in the accounts of guns being made. Two-part cannon are included in an inventory of 1509. In 1512 the works were taken over by Humphrey Walker, the King's gunfounder, followed by a succession of tenants which included Sir Thomas Boleyn in 1525. An account, probably of 1539 indicates that this furnace was very small, with only 160 tons' annual production. The furnace was in a state of decay by 1539, leading to a new furnace being built on the west side of Ashdown Forest. The forge remained in good repair. In 1574 Henry Bowyer had a royal furnace and forge in Ashdown Forest; in one version of the lists drawn up that year this is identified as a double furnace at Newbridge. It was last noted as working in 1603.

The pond is dry. The bay is about 180m long and 3m high on the down-stream side. It is breached by the road and the mill leat. At the eastern end of the bay, east of the road, earthworks may relate to later use. There is a working

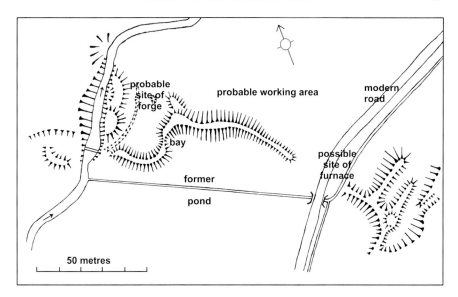

75 Newbridge furnace plan (*R. Houghton*)

area at the western end, adjacent to the stream and spillway but separated from it by a semi-circular length of the bay which contains remains of two probable wheel pits which may have been related to the forge. Large quantities of glassy slag were observed in the grounds of the cottage north of the site.

MUSEUMS

Anne of Cleves House Museum, 52, Southover High Street, Lewes, East Sussex, BN7 1JA
The Iron Gallery explains aspects of the industry through reconstructions, such as a gun-casting pit, and a cannon-boring rig based on remains found at the Pippingford furnaces. Many artefacts include an impressive collection of firebacks.

Hastings Museum & Art Gallery, John's Place, Bohemia Road, Hastings, East Sussex, TN34 1ET
The museum's important collection of firebacks, as well as other artefacts relating to the iron industry, have been put into store following reorganisation of the galleries.

Victoria & Albert Museum, Cromwell Road, South Kensington, London, SW7 2RL
The Metalwork Gallery has a fine collection of iron firebacks, many of them from the Weald, and a section of the railings from St Paul's Cathedral.

Royal Armouries Artillery Museum, Fort Nelson, Portsdown Hill Road, Fareham, Hampshire, PO17 6AN
Traces the history and development of artillery. The collection includes many examples of cannon cast in the Weald, as well as a reconstruction of cannon casting.

Guildford Museum, Castle Arch, Quarry Street, Guildford, Surrey, GU1 3SX
Small display of artefacts associated with iron-making in Surrey, including a number of iron firebacks.

Petworth House, Petworth, West Sussex, GU28 0AE (National Trust)
The Slade Mitford collection of iron firebacks is displayed in the former servants' quarters. The firebacks are predominantly of continental origin.

Horsham Museum, 9, Causeway, Horsham, West Sussex, RH12 1HE
Small display of artefacts associated with iron-making, including a couple of firebacks and a pair of well-preserved, early eighteenth-century cannon cast at Brede furnace.

Rottingdean Grange, The Green, Rottingdean, Brighton, BN2 7HA
A small collection of firebacks, including one of only three surviving wooden fireback patterns (the others being at Anne of Cleves House, Lewes).

CHURCHES WITH IRON GRAVE SLABS

Kent
Chiddingstone – aisles (3)
Cowden – nave and churchyard (3)
Foots Cray – churchyard (1)
Horsmonden – choir (1)

Surrey
Crowhurst – chancel (1)

East Sussex
Brightling – churchyard and porch (6)
Burwash – chapel wall (1)
Crowhurst – (concealed) (1)
East Grinstead – nave and aisle wall (3)
Frant – (concealed) (3)
Hartfield – aisle (1)
Laughton – tower (2)

Maresfield – tower (1)
Mayfield – nave and choir (concealed) (8)
Penhurst – (concealed) (1)
Rotherfield – aisle (1)
Salehurst – tower (7)
Sedlescombe – aisle (1)
Streat – nave (2)
Ticehurst – side chapel (1)
Uckfield – aisle wall (1)
Wadhurst – nave, aisles, choir, porch, churchyard (33)
Withyham – chancel and churchyard (2)

Essex
Rivenhall – nave (1)

London
Bermondsey – aisle (1)

West Sussex
West Hoathly – aisle walls and chancel (4)

APPENDIX 2

LIST OF BLAST FURNACES AND FINERY FORGES

Sites marked with an asterisk★ can be viewed from public roads, bridleways or footpaths, depending upon the vegetation at the time of year. GF denotes a former gunfoundry.

Please note, no right of access to any site is implied by the information available in this list. If you are interested in visiting a site, you must ensure that you have the permission of the landowner and/or tenant.

Abinger	Surrey	
Abinger Hammer★	Forge	TQ 097474
Ardingly	**West Sussex**	
Ardingly Forge	Forge	TQ 334289
Ardingly Furnace★	Furnace	TQ 337287
Strudgate Furnace★	Furnace	TQ 329323
Ashburnham	**East Sussex**	
Kitchenham Forge★	Forge	TQ 679135
Ashburnham (Upper) Forge★	Forge	TQ 687161
Ashurst	**Kent**	
Ashurst Forge 2	Forge	TQ 507391
Ashurst Furnace★	Furnace GF	TQ 507390
Battle	**East Sussex**	
Beech Mill★	Furnace GF	TQ 728167
Netherfield Furnace★	Furnace	TQ 721170
Beckley	**East Sussex**	
Beckley (Conster) Furnace★	Furnace Forge GF	TQ 836212
Bexhill	**East Sussex**	
Buckholt Forge	Forge Furnace	TQ 746113
Bidborough	**Kent**	
Barden Furnace★	Furnace GF	TQ 548424
Biddenden	**Kent**	
Biddenden Hammer Mill★	Forge Furnace	TQ 822383

Bramshott	Hampshire	
Bramshott Hammer	Forge	SU 819344
Brede	**East Sussex**	
Brede Furnace	Furnace GF	TQ 801192
Brenchley	**Kent**	
Horsmonden (Brenchley) Furnace★	Furnace GF	TQ 695412
Brightling	**East Sussex**	
Socknersh Furnace★	Furnace	TQ 705233
Glazier's (Brightling) Forge★	Forge	TQ 651213
Burwash	**East Sussex**	
Burwash Forge★	Forge	TQ 663231
Broadhurst Furnace	Furnace	TQ 631242
Buxted	**East Sussex**	
Little Forge★	Forge Furnace	TQ 513260
Oldlands Furnace	Furnace	TQ 477272
Iron Plat (Queenstock) Furnace	Furnace Forge GF	TQ 499242
Capel	**Kent**	
Postern Forge★	Forge	TQ 606462
Rats Castle Forge	Forge	TQ 612468
Catsfield	**East Sussex**	
Potmans Forge★	Forge	TQ 725117
Catsfield Furnace★	Furnace	TQ 732115
Chiddingfold	**Surrey**	
Imbhams Furnace★	Furnace GF	SU 932329
West End Furnace★	Furnace	SU 939345
Chiddingly	**East Sussex**	
Stream Mill★	Furnace GF Forge	TQ 555155
Chithurst	**West Sussex**	
Chithurst (Iping) Forge★	Forge	SU 846236
Cowden	**Kent**	
Prinkham Farm Forge	Forge	TQ 494409
Scarlets Furnace★	Furnace GF	TQ 442400
Cowden Furnace★	Furnace GF	TQ 454400
Cranbrook	**Kent**	
Bedgebury Furnace★	Furnace GF	TQ 739347
Cranleigh	**Surrey**	
Vachery Forge★	Forge	TQ 062370
Vachery Furnace	Furnace	TQ 071375
Crawley	**West Sussex**	
Ifield Forge★	Forge	TQ 245365
Blackwater Green Forge	Forge	TQ 292363
Tinsley Forge	Forge	TQ 291395

Tilgate Furnace	Furnace	TQ 284355
Crowhurst	**East Sussex**	
Crowhurst Furnace★	Furnace Forge	TQ 757122
Cuckfield Rural	**West Sussex**	
Cuckfield Forge	Forge	TQ 302235
Blackfold Furnace★	Furnace	TQ 274294
Cuckfield Furnace★	Furnace	TQ 304230
Holmsted (Gastons Bridge) Forge★	Forge	TQ 282274
Duncton	**West Sussex**	
Burton Forge★	Forge	SU 979180
Dunsfold	**Surrey**	
Burningfold Forge & Furnace★	Forge Furnace GF	TQ 004343
East Grinstead	**West Sussex**	
Stone Furnace	Furnace Forge	TQ 382343
Mill Place Furnace★	Furnace	TQ 374349
Etchingham	**East Sussex**	
Darfold Furnace★	Furnace	TQ 701280
Etchingham Forge★	Forge	TQ 701266
Burgh Wood Forge★	Forge	TQ 717276
Ewhurst	**East Sussex**	
Ewhurst Furnace★	Furnace	TQ 810248
Fernhurst	**West Sussex**	
Verdley Wood Furnace★	Furnace	SU 906265
Fletching	**East Sussex**	
Fletching Forge★	Forge	TQ 424229
Sheffield Furnace★	Furnace	TQ 416257
Sheffield Forge	Forge	TQ 404238
Forest Row	**East Sussex**	
Brambletye Forge★	Forge	TQ 414350
Bower Forge	Forge	TQ 441384
Framfield	**East Sussex**	
Tickerage Furnace★	Furnace	TQ 515211
New Place Furnace★	Furnace	TQ 509195
Pounsley Furnace	Furnace GF	TQ 529219
Frant	**East Sussex**	
Henly (Upper) Furnace	?Furnace	TQ 601338
Benhall Forge★	Forge	TQ 608376
Henly (Brinklaw) Furnace★	Furnace	TQ 602336
Breechers (Marriotts Croft) Forge★	Forge	TQ 627384
Tollslye Furnace	Furnace	TQ 632371
Eridge Forge★	Forge	TQ 560350
Eridge Furnace	Furnace	TQ 564350
High Rocks (Hungershall) Forge	Forge	TQ 557382

Brookland Forge	Forge Bloomery	TQ 618349
Verredge Forge★	Forge	TQ 621352
Riverhall Furnace	Furnace Forge GF	TQ 608335
Godstone	**Surrey**	
Woodcock Hammer★	Forge Wiremill	TQ 369419
Goudhurst	**Kent**	
Chingley Forge	Forge	TQ 682335
Chingley Furnace	Furnace	TQ 685327
Bedgebury Forge	Forge	TQ 727357
Hadlow Down	**East Sussex**	
Howbourne Forge★	Forge	TQ 515250
Huggetts Furnace★	Furnace GF	TQ 534260
Hartfield	**East Sussex**	
Steel Forge	Steel Forge	TQ 450316
Newbridge Furnace★ (see Appendix 1)	Furnace GF Forge	TQ 456325
Cansiron Forge★	Forge ?Furnace	TQ 453383
Cotchford Forge★	Forge	TQ 470339
Parrock Furnace★	Furnace Forge	TQ 458357
Pippingford Furnace	Furnace (2) GF	TQ 450316
Bassetts Furnace★	Furnace	TQ 468374
Harting	**West Sussex**	
Habin Forge	Forge	SU 800224
Haslemere	**Surrey**	
Sturt Hammer	Forge Sicklemill	SU 887325
Pophole Hammer★	Forge	SU 874326
Hawkhurst	**Kent**	
Hawkhurst Furnace★	Furnace GF Forge	TQ 774313
Frith Furnace★	Furnace	TQ 736325
Heathfield	**East Sussex**	
Heathfield Furnace	Furnace GF	TQ 599187
Bungehurst Furnace	Furnace	TQ 559235
Herstmonceux	**East Sussex**	
Batsford Furnace	Furnace GF	TQ 631153
Cowbeech (Cralle) Furnace★	Furnace Forge	TQ 612151
Hever	**Kent**	
Bough Beech (Chiddingstone) Furnace 2★	Furnace GF	TQ 481476
Bough Beech Furnace 1★	Furnace	TQ 481475
Horam	**East Sussex**	
Waldron Furnace★	Furnace GF	TQ 566181
Horsham	**West Sussex**	
Warnham Furnace★	Furnace	TQ 168323

Horsted Keynes	West Sussex	
Freshfield Forge★	Forge	TQ 386245
Horsted Keynes Furnace★	Furnace	TQ 379287
Kirdford	West Sussex	
Ebernoe Furnace★ (see Appendix 1)	Furnace	SU 976277
Shillinglee Furnace★	Furnace ?GF	SU 972308
Wassell Forge★	Forge	SU 981281
Barkfold (Idehurst) Forge	Forge	TQ 029259
Roundwick Furnace	Furnace	SU 992287
Barkfold Furnace★	Furnace	TQ 030269
Lamberhurst	Kent	
Gloucester Furnace★	Furnace GF	TQ 661359
Bayham Forge	Forge	TQ 642366
Hoadly Forge	Forge	TQ 662361
Leigh	Surrey	
Leigh Hammer★	Forge	TQ 222461
Linchmere	West Sussex	
Northpark (Fernhurst) Furnace★	Furnace GF	SU 878283
Lower Beeding	West Sussex	
St Leonards Upper Forge★	Forge	TQ 219289
Gosden Furnace	Furnace	TQ 229251
Bewbush Furnace★	Furnace	TQ 239357
St Leonards Lower Forge	Forge Furnace	TQ 213291
Lurgashall	West Sussex	
Lurgashall Furnace	Furnace	SU 942261
Maresfield	East Sussex	
Hendall Furnace and Forge★	Furnace Forge GF	TQ 471259
Maresfield Furnace★	Furnace GF	TQ 462232
Stumbletts Furnace	Furnace	TQ 399306
Langley (Langles) Furnace	Furnace GF Forge	TQ 451239
Old Forge (Marshalls Furnace)	Furnace GF Forge	TQ 459258
Maresfield Forge	Forge	TQ 460228
Mayfield	East Sussex	
Woolbridge Forge★	Bloomery Forge	TQ 571266
Old Mill Furnace★	Furnace	TQ 588245
Bivelham (Bibleham) Forge★	Forge	TQ 641266
Mayfield Furnace★	Furnace GF Boring Mill	TQ 593282
Moat Mill Forge★	Forge	TQ 592251
Hawksden Forge★	Forge Furnace	TQ 623266
Mayfield Forge★	Forge	TQ 594281
Coushopley Furnace★	Furnace	TQ 604302

Milland	West Sussex	
Milland Furnace	Furnace	SU 832281
Mountfield	**East Sussex**	
Hodesdale Forge★	Forge	TQ 748183
Mountfield Furnace and Forge★	Forge Furnace	TQ 749196
Darwell (Darvel) Furnace	Furnace GF	TQ 708207
Newdigate	**Surrey**	
Ewood Furnace★	Furnace Forge	TQ 201447
Northchapel	**West Sussex**	
Frith Furnace★	Furnace	SU 955309
Mitchell Park Forge★	Forge	SU 977297
Northiam	**East Sussex**	
Northiam Furnace★	Furnace	TQ 817245
Nuthurst	**West Sussex**	
Birchenbridge Forge★	Forge	TQ 193292
Pembury	**Kent**	
Melhill Forge	Forge	TQ 615381
Dundle Forge★	Forge	TQ 629385
Penhurst	**East Sussex**	
Ashburnham Furnace★	Furnace GF	TQ 686171
Penhurst Furnace★	Furnace	TQ 705163
Panningridge Furnace	Furnace	TQ 687174
Rogate	**West Sussex**	
Coombe Furnace★	Furnace	SU 815269
Rotherfield	**East Sussex**	
Birchden Forge★	Forge	TQ 533353
Maynards Gate Furnace	Furnace GF	TQ 539298
Maynards Gate Forge	Forge	TQ 540298
Hamsell Furnace★	Furnace GF	TQ 538344
Cowford Furnace★	Furnace	TQ 559320
Rudgwick	**West Sussex**	
Dedisham Furnace★	Furnace	TQ 107333
Dedisham Forge	Forge	TQ 103329
Salehurst	**East Sussex**	
Bugsell Forge★	Forge	TQ 724256
Iridge Furnace	Furnace	TQ 749277
Robertsbridge Abbey Forge★	Forge Steel Forge	TQ 756236
Robertsbridge Furnace★	Furnace GF	TQ 751231
Sandhurst	**Kent**	
Boxhurst Steel Forge	Steel Forge	Not known
Shipley	**West Sussex**	
Shipley Forge★	Forge	TQ 149208
Knepp Furnace	Furnace	TQ 163211

Slaugham	West Sussex	
Slaugham Furnace★	Furnace	TQ 249285
Southborough	**Kent**	
Vauxhall Furnace	Furnace	TQ 592440
Old Forge, Southborough	Forge	TQ 594428
Stedham	**West Sussex**	
Inholmes Copse Furnace	Furnace	SU 855263
Thursley	**Surrey**	
Thursley Lower Hammer★	Forge	SU 916408
Thursley Upper Hammer★	Forge	SU 916403
Coldharbour (Horsebane) Hammer	Forge	SU 920406
Ticehurst	**East Sussex**	
Pashley Furnace	Furnace	TQ 710295
East Lymden Furnace	Furnace	TQ 677291
Turners Hill	**West Sussex**	
Worth Forest Furnace	Furnace GF	TQ 290335
Wadhurst	**East Sussex**	
Scrag Oak (Snape) Furnace	Furnace	TQ 637297
Warbleton	**East Sussex**	
Steel Forge	Forge Steel Forge	TQ 604170
Warbleton Priory Furnace★	Furnace	TQ 644174
Markly Furnace★	Furnace	TQ 624183
Woodman's Forge	?Forge ?Furnace	TQ 603176
West Hoathly	**West Sussex**	
Chittingly Furnace	Furnace	TQ 346322
Gravetye Furnace	Furnace GF	TQ 366342
Westfield	**East Sussex**	
Westfield (Crowham) Forge★	Forge	TQ 814172
Wisborough Green	**West Sussex**	
Pallingham Furnace★	Furnace	TQ 041227
Withyham	**East Sussex**	
Crowborough (Grubsbars) Forge★	Forge	TQ 498326
Withyham Forge	Forge	TQ 500353
Crowborough Warren (Withyham) Furnace★ (see Appendix 1)	Furnace	TQ 496322
Ashurst (Pilbeams) Forge	Forge	TQ 505403
Witley	**Surrey**	
Witley Park Furnace	Furnace	SU 927374

Worth	West Sussex	
Rowfant Forge★	Forge	TQ 316378
Rowfant Supra Forge	Forge	TQ 319372
Warren Furnace★	Furnace GF	TQ 348393

SELECT BIBLIOGRAPHY

Aldridge, N., (2001) 'Ironworking sites in the Weald of Kent', *Wealden Iron*, 2nd ser., 21, 9-14

Awty, B.G., (1981) 'The continental origins of Wealden ironworkers, 1451-1544', *Economic History Review*, 2nd ser., 34, 524-539

Awty, B.G. & Whittick, C.H.C., (2002) 'The lordship of Canterbury, iron-founding at Buxted, and the continental antecedents of cannon-founding in the Weald', *Sussex Archaeological Collections*, 140, 71-81

Baines, J.M., (1958) *Wealden Firebacks*, Hastings Museum

Barter Bailey, S., (2000) *Prince Rupert's Patent Guns*, Leeds, Royal Armouries

Bedwin, O.R., (1976) 'The excavation of Ardingly Fulling Mill and Forge, 1975-76', *Post-Medieval Archaeology*, 10, 34-64

Bedwin, O.R., (1978) 'The excavation of a late sixteenth/early seventeenth-century blast furnace at Maynard's Gate, Crowborough, East Sussex, 1975-76', *Sussex Archaeological Collections*, 116, 163-178

Bedwin, O.R., (1980) 'The excavation of a late 16th-century blast furnace at Batsford, Herstmonceux, East Sussex, 1978', *Post-Medieval Archaeology*, 14, 89-112

Beswick, W.R., Broomhall, P.J. & Bickersteth, J.D., (1984) 'Ashburnham blast furnace: a definitive date for its closure', *Sussex Archaeological Collections*, 122, 226-227

Beswick, W.R., (2003) 'The excavation of a first-century ironworks at Turners Green, Sussex, 1968-70', *Wealden Iron*, 2nd ser., 23, 6-21

Brandon, P. (2003) *The Kent & Sussex Weald*, Chichester, Phillimore

Brodribb, G. & Cleere, H.F., (1988) 'The Classis Britannica Bath-house at Beauport Park, East Sussex', *Britannia*, 19, 218-274

Brown, R.R., (1989) 'Identifying 18th-century trunnion marks on British iron guns: a discussion', *International Journal of Nautical Archaeology and Underwater Exploration*, 18, 4, 321-329

Brown, R.R., (1993) 'Notes on Wealden furnaces – Board of Ordnance records 1660-1700', *Wealden Iron*, 2nd ser., 13, 20-30

Brown, R.R., (1994) 'Wealden ironmasters and the Board of Ordnance after 1770', *Wealden Iron*, 2nd ser., 14, 31-47

Brown, R.R., (1999) 'Notes from the Board of Ordnance papers 1705-1720', *Wealden Iron*, 2nd ser., 19, 34-46

Brown, R.R., (2000) 'Notes from the Office of Ordnance: the 1650s', *Wealden Iron*, 2nd ser., 20, 39-55

Brown, R.R., (2001) 'Thomas Westerne: the Great Ironmonger', *Journal of the Ordnance Society*, 13, 39-53

Brown, R.R., (2001) 'Extracts from the Debenture Books of the Office of Ordnance 1593-1610', *Wealden Iron*, 2nd ser., 21, 14-20

Brown, R.R., (2004) 'The Ordnance records: Thomas Browne', *Wealden Iron*, 2nd ser., 24, 16-25

Brown, R.R., (2005) 'John Browne, gunfounder to the Stuarts', *Wealden Iron*, 2nd ser., 25, 38-61

Brown, R.R., (2006) 'John Browne, gunfounder to the Stuarts; part 2: bronze and iron guns 1630-45', *Wealden Iron*, 2nd ser., 26, 31-50

Butler, D., (1981) 'The Fullers and Carron', *Wealden Iron*, 2nd ser., 1, 24-31

Campbell, R.H., (1961) *Carron Company*, Edinburgh, Oliver & Boyd

Cartwright, C., (1992) 'The excavation of a Romano-British ironworking site at Broadfield, Crawley, West Sussex', *Sussex Archaeological Collections*, 130, 22-59

Cattell, C.S., (1971) 'An evaluation of the Loseley list of ironworks within the Weald in the year 1588', *Archaeologia Cantiana*, 86, 85-92

Cleere, H.F., (1970) *The Romano-British Industrial Site at Bardown, Wadhurst*, Sussex Archaeological Society Occasional Paper 1

Cleere. H.F., (1974) 'The Roman Iron Industry of the Weald and its Connexions with the Classis Britannica', *Archaeological Journal*, 131, 171-199

Cleere, H.F., (1976) 'Some operating parameters for Roman ironworks', *Bulletin of the Institute of Archaeology*, 13, 233-246

Cleere, H.F. & Crossley, D.W., (1995) *The Iron Industry of the Weald*, Cardiff, Merton Priory Press

Chown, E., (1947) 'Painted Iron Age pottery at Sedlescombe', *Sussex Notes & Queries*, 11, 7, 148-151

Crocker, G., (1999) 'Seventeenth-Century Wireworks in Surrey and the Case of Thomas Steere', *Surrey History*, 6, 1, 2-16

Crossley, D.W., (1966) 'The management of a sixteenth-century ironworks', *Economic History Review*, 2nd ser., 19, 272-288

Crossley, D.W., (1972) 'A sixteenth-century Wealden blast furnace: a report on excavations at Panningridge, Sussex, 1964-70', *Post-Medieval Archaeology*, 6, 42-68

Crossley, D.W., (1974) 'Ralph Hogge's ironworks accounts, 1576-81', *Sussex Archaeological Collections*, 112, 48-79

Crossley, D.W., (1975) *Sidney Ironworks Accounts 1541-1573*, Royal Historical Society, Camden, 4th ser., 15

Crossley, D.W., (1975) *The Bewl Valley Ironworks*, London, Royal Archaeological Institute

Crossley, D.W., (1975) 'Cannon-manufacture at Pippingford, Sussex: the excavation of two iron furnaces of c.1717', *Post-Medieval Archaeology*, 9, 1-37

Crossley, D.W., (1979) 'A gun-casting furnace at Scarlets, Cowden, Kent', *Post-Medieval Archaeology*, 13, 239-249

Crossley, D.W. & Saville, R.V., (1991) *The Fuller Letters 1728-1755: Guns, Slaves and Finance*, Lewes, Sussex Record Society, vol. 76

De Beer, C., (1991) *The Art of Gunfounding: The Casting of Bronze Cannon in the Late Eighteenth Century*, Rotherfield, Jean Boudriot Publications

Dodson, J.G., (1863) 'On some old Acts of Parliament concerning roads in, or connected with, the county of Sussex', *Sussex Archaeological Collections*, 15, 138-147

Gallois, R.W., (1965) *British Regional Geology: The Wealden District*, London, HMSO

Gillespie, C.C. (ed.), (1993) *A Diderot Pictorial Encyclopedia of Trades and Industry*, New York, Dover

Giuseppi, M.S., (1902) 'The Manor of Ewood and the ironworks there in 1575', *Surrey Archaeological Collections*, 17, 28-40

Giuseppi, M.S., (1912) 'The accounts of the ironworks at Sheffield and Worth in Sussex, 1546-1549', *Archaeological Journal*, 69, 276-311

Giuseppi, M.S., (1913) 'Some Fourteenth-Century Accounts of Ironworks at Tudeley, Kent', *Archaeologia*, 64, 145-164

Hammer, F., (2003) *Industry in north-west Roman Southwark*, Museum of London Archaeological Service Monograph 17

Hodgkinson, J.S., (1985) 'A Romano-British ironworking site at Crawley Down, Worth, Sussex', *Wealden Iron*, 2nd ser., 5, 9-20

Hodgkinson, J.S., (1987) 'Footlands ironworking site, Sedlescombe', *Wealden Iron*, 2nd ser., 7, 25-32

Hodgkinson, J.S., (1987) 'Iron ore extraction – an eighteenth-century example', *Wealden Iron*, 2nd ser., 7, 35-37

Hodgkinson, J.S., (1989) 'William Clutton - ironmaster', *Wealden Iron*, 2nd ser., 9, 27-33

Hodgkinson, J.S., (1995) 'Notes on early-eighteenth century memoranda on the making of iron', *Wealden Iron*, 2nd ser., 15, 9-18

Hodgkinson, J.S., (1996) 'The decline in the ordnance trade in the Weald', *Sussex Archaeological Collections*, 134, 155-167

Hodgkinson, J.S., (1996) 'Fourteenth century ironworks in Wartling Manor', *Wealden Iron*, 2nd ser., 16, 7-9

Hodgkinson, J.S., (1997) 'Forges in the late-eighteenth century Weald', *Wealden Iron*, 2nd ser., 17, 13-23

Hodgkinson, J.S., (1999) 'Romano-British iron production in the Sussex and Kent Weald: a review of current data', *Historical Metallurgy*, 33, 2, 68-72

Hodgkinson, J.S., (2000) 'The Raby Background: The Midlands, London and the Weald', in Crocker, G., *Alexander Raby, Ironmaster*, Guildford, Surrey Industrial History Group

Hodgkinson, J.S., (2000) 'A gazetteer of medieval iron-making sites in the Weald', *Wealden Iron*, 2nd ser., 20, 23-32

Hodgkinson, J.S., (2002) 'Factors of production in mid-eighteenth century Wealden iron smelting', *Wealden Iron*, 2nd ser., 22, 36-56

Hodgkinson, J. S., (2004) 'Iron production in Surrey', 233-244, in Cotton, J., Crocker, G. & Graham, A., *Aspects of Archaeology & History in Surrey*, Guildford, Surrey Archaeological Society

Hodgkinson, J.S., (2004) 'Ironworks in late-sixteenth century Kent', *Wealden Iron*, 2nd ser., 24, 6-16

Hodgkinson, J.S., (2007) 'A godly chimney plate and other firebacks from Brede', *Wealden Iron*, 2nd ser., 27, 18-26

Hodgkinson, J.S. & Houghton, R.G., (1997) 'Ebernoe furnace – site survey 1996', *Wealden Iron*, 2nd ser., 17, 9-13

Hodgkinson, J.S. & Whittick, C.H.C., (1998) 'The Tudeley ironworks accounts', *Wealden Iron*, 2nd ser., 18, 7-38

Houghton, R.G., (1997) 'A reconstruction of a Wealden conversion forge and boring mill', *Wealden Iron*, 2nd ser., 17, 23-40

Houghton, R.G., (2006) 'The construction of a Wealden blast furnace', *Wealden Iron*, 2nd ser., 26, 10-30

Kenyon, G.H., (1969) 'Piper's Copse Camp, Northchapel', *Sussex Notes & Queries*, 17, 3, 105

Ketteringham, L.L., (1976) *Alsted: Excavation of a Thirteenth-Fourteenth Sub-Manor House with its Ironworks in Netherne Wood, Merstham, Surrey*, Guildford, Surrey Archaeological Society Research Vol. 2

King, P.W., (1995) 'Ashburnham furnace in the early eighteenth century', *Sussex Archaeological Collections*, 133, 255-262

King, P.W., (2002) 'Bar iron production in the Weald in the early eighteenth century', *Wealden Iron*, 2nd ser., 22, 26-34

Lemmon, C.H. & Darrell Hill, J., (1966) 'The Romano-British site at Bodiam', *Sussex Archaeological Collections*, 104, 88-102

Lower, M.A., (1849) 'Ironworks of the county of Sussex', *Sussex Archaeological Collections*, 2, 169-220

Magilton, J., (ed.) (2003) *Fernhurst Furnace*, Chichester, Chichester District Archaeology 2

Margary, I.D., (1965) *Roman Ways in the Weald*, London, Dent

Marshall, P., (1958) 'The Diary of Sir James Hope', *Miscellany Vol. 9*, Scottish History Society, 3rd ser., 50, 129-197

Meades, D.M., (1988) 'Langles Furnace and Forge Site Survey 1986/7', *Wealden Iron*, 2nd ser., 8, 48-53

Millett, M., (2007) 'Roman Kent' in Williams, J.H., *The Archaeology of Kent to AD 800*, Woodbridge, Boydell & Kent County Council

Money, J.H., (1971) 'Medieval Ironworkings in Minepit Wood, Rotherfield, Sussex', *Medieval Archaeology*, 15, 86-111

Money, J.H., (1974) 'Iron age and Romano-British ironworking site in Minepit Wood, Rotherfield, Sussex', *Journal of the Historical Metallurgy Society*, 8, 1, 1-20

Money, J.H., (1977) 'The Iron Age hill-fort and Romano-British ironworking settlement at Garden Hill, Sussex', *Britannia*, 8, 339-350

Paynter, S., (2006) 'Regional variations in bloomery smelting slag of the Iron Age and Romano-British periods', *Archaeometry*, 48, 2, 271-292

Paynter, S., (2007) 'Romano-British workshops for iron smelting and smithing at Westhawk Farm, Kent', *Historical Metallurgy*, 41, 1, 15-31

Place, C. & Bedwin, O.R., (1992) 'The sixteenth-century forge at Blackwater Green, Worth, Crawley, West Sussex: excavations 1988', *Sussex Archaeological Collections*, 130, 147-163

Pleiner, R., (2000) *Iron in Archaeology: The European Bloomery Smelters*, Prague, Archeologický Ústav Avčr

Rock, J., (1879) 'Ancient Cinderheaps in East Sussex', *Sussex Archaeological Collections*, 29, 167-180

Rostoker, W. & Bronson, B., (1990) *Pre-industrial iron: its technology and ethnology*, Archeomaterials monographs, no. 1, Philadelphia

Salzman, L.F., (1915) 'Some Sussex Domesday Tenants', *Sussex Archaeological Collections*, 57, 162-179

Saville, R.V., (1980) 'The operation of charcoal blast furnaces in Sussex in the early eighteenth century', *Historical Metallurgy*, 14, 2, 65-73

Saville, R.V., (1982) 'Income and production at Heathfield ironworks, 1693-1788', *Wealden Iron*, 2nd ser., 2, 36-63

Schubert, H.R., (1952) 'The first English blast furnace', *Journal of the Iron & Steel Institute*, 170, 108-110

Schubert, H.R., (1957) *History of the British iron and Steel Industry*, London, Routledge

Straker, E., (1931) *Wealden Iron*, London, Bell

Straker, E. & Lucas, B.H., (1938) 'A Romano-British bloomery in East Sussex', *Sussex Archaeological Collections*, 79, 224-232

Tebbutt, C.F., (1972) 'A Roman bloomery at Great Cansiron, near Holtye, Sussex', *Sussex Archaeological Collections*, 110, 10-13

Tebbutt, C.F., (1975) 'An abandoned medieval industrial site at Parrock, Hartfield', *Sussex Archaeological Collections*, 113, 146-151

Tebbutt, C.F., (1982) 'A Middle-Saxon iron smelting site at Millbrook, Ashdown Forest, Sussex', *Sussex Archaeological Collections*, 120, 19-35

Teesdale, E.B., (1984) *The Queen's Gunstonemaker*, Seaford, Lindel

Teesdale, E.B., (1991) *Gunfounding in the Weald in the sixteenth century*, London, Royal Armouries

Tomlinson, H.C., (1976) 'Wealden gunfounding: an analysis of its demise in the eighteenth century', *Economic History Review*, 2nd ser., 29, 383-400

Tylecote, R.F., (1986) *The Prehistory of Metallurgy in the British Isles*, London, Institute of Metals

Whittick, C.H.C., (1992) 'Wealden iron in California – the Huntington Library', *Wealden Iron*, 2nd ser., 12, 29-62

Willatts, R.M., (1987) 'Iron graveslabs: a sideline of the early iron industry', *Sussex Archaeological Collections*, 125, 99-113

Willatts, R.M., (1988) 'Pre-Industrial Revolution cast-iron graveslabs', *Wealden Iron*, 2nd ser., 8, 12-47

Williams, L.J., (1959) 'A Carmarthenshire ironmaster and the Seven Years' War', *Business History*, 2, 32-43

Worssam, B. & Swift, G., (1987) 'Minepits at West Hoathly Brickworks, Sharpthorne, Sussex', *Wealden Iron*, 2nd ser., 7, 3-15

ABOUT THE AUTHOR

A resident of the Weald for most of his life, Jeremy Hodgkinson is a retired teacher who has written and lectured on the Wealden iron industry for thirty years. He gained his MA in Regional and Local History from the University of Brighton in 1993 and was Chairman of the Wealden Iron Research Group from 1981–2005. He is a Fellow of the Society of Antiquaries of London.

INDEX